CAPE TOWN
THE CITY AT A GLANCE

Company's Garden
Planted by Dutch settlers in 1652, the park and vital green lung is surrounded by institutions of government and c...

Robben Island
Now a museum and heritage site – with more than 132 species of bird life – the island was most infamously a political prison, its inmates including Nelson Mandela.

Cape Town Stadium
Built for the 2010 World Cup, this unmissable arena has been criminally underused since.
See p010

City Hall
It was here, on 11 February 1990, that Nelson Mandela made his first speech after his release from prison. It's now a cultural centre.
Darling Street, T 021 465 2029

V&A Waterfront
After extensive redevelopment, which finished in 2006, these basins have become a thriving, if uninspiring, retail and dining destination.

Railway Station
This 1950s transport hub has been sensitively restored and the original windows remain.
Adderley Street

Castle of Good Hope
William Fehr's collection of decorative arts makes this 1679 fortress worth a visit.
Castle Street, T 021 787 1260

Civic Centre
Councillors meet in the revamped podium building, which has a bold shuttlecock-shaped roof, located beside the older concrete slab.
See p076

INTRODUCTION
THE CHANGING FACE OF THE URBAN SCENE

Due to Cape Town's jaw-dropping setting below Table Mountain, one of the world's natural wonders, its miles of unspoilt coast and winelands for satellite suburbs, you could fall for the city on looks alone. But this obscures the fact that it is also smoothly functional. If that weren't enough, in 2014 Cape Town assumes the mantle of World Design Capital, reflecting a vibrancy that has returned to the centre from Woodstock, the aspiring arts district. By then, Portside, a 139m tower by architects Dhk and Louis Karol, will be the city's tallest building, adding to the cosmopolitan character of the CBD, which is defined by its modish bars, stylish galleries and boutiques, fine dining and café culture. Delightful places to stay abound, from remnants of white-mischief colonial glamour to the avant-garde. And in summer, the insouciant beach enclave of Camps Bay turns into South Africa's party hub. However, nothing is obligatory, the word 'chill' being part of every Capetonian's vocabulary.

Two decades into democratic rule and with a successful FIFA World Cup in the bag, the city is in cruise mode. But even though apartheid is gone, inequality takes much longer to unravel – a fact plainly apparent shortly after you land. The townships, such as the ones near the airport, are home to a vast black underclass. So there remains a gritty edginess here, yet there is also a palpable optimism and the belief that Cape Town is heading in the right direction. And it's a ride you really shouldn't miss.

ESSENTIAL INFO
FACTS, FIGURES AND USEFUL ADDRESSES

TOURIST OFFICE
Pinnacle Building
Burg Street/Castle Street
T 021 487 6800
www.capetown.travel

TRANSPORT
Airport transfer to city centre
www.centuriontours.co.za
The journey takes roughly 20 minutes
Car hire
African Welcome
T 021 934 4004
Helicopter
Civair
T 021 934 4488
Taxis
Rikkis Taxis
T 0861 745 547
Calling for a taxi is advisable, although there are ranks in popular locations

EMERGENCY SERVICES
Emergencies
T 107 (from a landline)
T 021 480 7700 (from a mobile)
Late-night pharmacy (until 11pm)
Litekem Pharmacy
24 Darling Street
T 021 461 8040

CONSULATES
British Consulate General
15th floor, Norton Rose House
8 Riebeeck Street
T 021 405 2400
www.ukinsouthafrica.fco.gov.uk
US Consulate General
2 Reddam Avenue
Westlake
T 021 702 7300
southafrica.usembassy.gov

POSTAL SERVICES
Post office
Loop Street/Pepper Street
T 021 464 7477
www.sapo.co.za
Shipping
DHL
T 0860 345 000

BOOKS
Modern Wineries of South Africa
by Hugh Fraser (Quivertree)
The Institute for Taxi Poetry by
Imraan Coovadia (Random House Struik)

WEBSITES
Architecture
www.saia.org.za
Art/Design
www.artthrob.co.za
www.designindaba.com
Newspaper
www.capetimes.co.za

EVENTS
Creative Week
www.creativeweekct.co.za
Stellenbosch Wine Festival
www.stellenboschwinefestival.co.za

COST OF LIVING
Taxi from Cape Town International Airport to city centre
R300
Cappuccino
R20
Packet of cigarettes
R20
Daily newspaper
R6.50
Bottle of champagne
R650

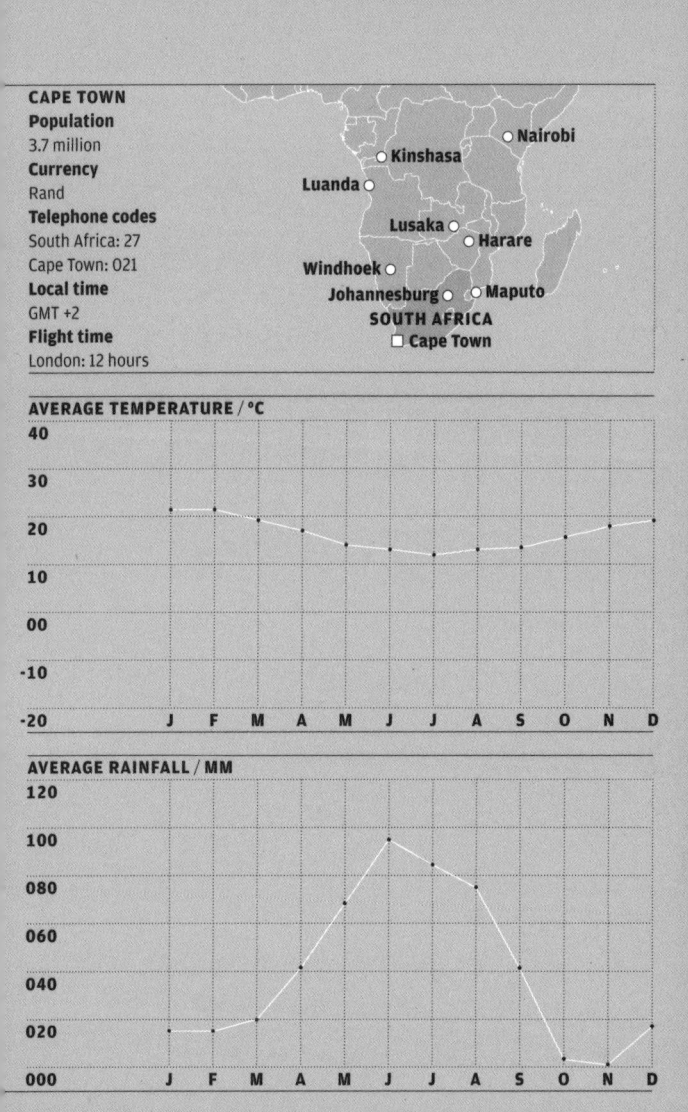

CAPE TOWN
Population
3.7 million
Currency
Rand
Telephone codes
South Africa: 27
Cape Town: 021
Local time
GMT +2
Flight time
London: 12 hours

AVERAGE TEMPERATURE / °C

AVERAGE RAINFALL / MM

NEIGHBOURHOODS
THE AREAS YOU NEED TO KNOW AND WHY

To help you navigate the city, we've chosen the most interesting districts (see the map inside the back cover) and underlined featured venues in colour, according to their location (see below); those venues that are outside these areas are not coloured.

ATLANTIC SEABOARD
Super-suburbs Camps Bay and Clifton are full of modernist villas and nightspots, including the glitzy St Yves Beach Club (see p046). Bantry Bay and Fresnaye are equally upmarket, if less energetic, and offer fantastic views but only slivers of beach. Sea Point is the area's poor cousin, but has a busy promenade that is good for a stroll. Sunsets all along this stretch of coast are straight out of central casting.

GREEN POINT
The arrival of Cape Town's graceful giant of a stadium (see p010) means that there's now no way you can miss Green Point. Nearby De Waterkant, formerly a Cape Malay neighbourhood, has a vibrant gay culture and the Cape Quarter precinct, with its interiors stores, eateries, bars and clubs. Granger Bay and its environs are gentrifying as the likes of fashionable dining destination Grand Café & Beach (see p058) draw the crowds.

CENTRE
An artery leading from the harbour up the mountain, Long Street has an edgy boho vibe and is a popular nightlife hub. To the west is Bo-Kaap, a Cape Malay district known for its colourful houses. Company's Garden is an unexpected haven, and the area around Greenmarket Square, notably Church Street, is worth visiting. Artists, designers, theatregoers and digital whizz-kids congregate in the East City.

WATERFRONT/LOWER CITY
The Victoria & Alfred Waterfront is one of the city's proudest achievements, a safe and successful retail and entertainment complex, although its Disneyfied Victoriana is rather cringeworthy. Skip the mall, be selective about the craft shops and visit Robben Island via the Mandela Gateway. On the Foreshore's reclaimed land sits the International Convention Centre (1 Lower Long Street, T 021 410 5000).

WOODSTOCK
The route to the southern suburbs, still rough-around-the-edges Woodstock has been impressively reborn. Sir Lowry Road has attracted some of South Africa's best contemporary art galleries, including Stevenson (see p038). Meanwhile, The Old Biscuit Mill and Woodstock Exchange (see p080) have transformed Albert Road into a bustling design district. While in the area, look out for Faith47's graffiti – it is wry, political and charmingly feminine.

CITY BOWL SUBURBS
Set on the lower slopes of Table Mountain (see p012) and Signal Hill, the chichi des-res suburbs of Gardens, Vredehoek, Oranjezicht, Higgovale and Tamboerskloof are home to boutique hotels and architect-designed residences. Kloof Street has many enticing emporiums, as well as some stylish cafés, such as Manna Epicure (see p052), and, further up the road, late-night haunts like The Power & The Glory (see p050).

LANDMARKS
THE SHAPE OF THE CITY SKYLINE

Elsewhere in the world you might navigate by skyscrapers, bridges and parks, but here nothing can compete with the kilometre-high rock bang in the middle of the city. Perversely, it can be disorienting. On the ground, it's hard to grasp that much of Cape Town is always on the other side of one peak or another. In the City Bowl, nestled in the crook of Table Mountain (see p012) and Lion's Head, you feel as if you're in a small town. Then you nip over Kloof Nek and the Atlantic Seaboard is revealed, with its beachside suburbs and a dozen more peaks, the Twelve Apostles, reaching along the coast. Scoot round the back of Table Mountain and more miles of suburbs stretch past Newlands (see p089), all the way to False Bay.

The city is not without manmade landmarks. The Castle of Good Hope (Castle Street, T 021 787 1260), a low-lying 1679 pentagon, marks the old seafront before the Foreshore was reclaimed from mother nature in the 1930s. The area is now home to the high-rises that define the CBD. There's the monumental vacancy of District Six, a multiracial quarter that was bulldozed during apartheid and is being developed into affordable housing. Standing out, however, are structures that have become enduring symbols almost in spite of themselves: the love-them or loathe-them Disa Park Towers (see p014), the ostentatious Rhodes Memorial (see p013) and the perfectly situated Cape Town Stadium (overleaf).

For full addresses, see Resources.

Cape Town Stadium

German practice GMP worked with Cape Town architects Louis Karol and Point to create this saucer-like oval, its glinting facade of woven fibreglass coated with Teflon. Its finest moment came in 2010 when 64,100 people witnessed Germany embarrass Diego Maradona's Argentina 4-0 in the FIFA World Cup quarter-final. The capacity has since been reduced to 55,000 and it's used as a music venue for touring supergroups, and as the home ground of football team Ajax Cape Town. Many locals still question why the huge sum of R4.5bn was spent on this folly, which is visible from much of the city, in the light of far more pressing social concerns. If you are attending an event here, pop by Italian deli Giovanni's (T 021 434 6893) on Main Road.
Vlei Road

LANDMARKS

Table Mountain

Pilots cruise past Table Mountain (sit on the right on most flights arriving into Cape Town) and it dominates every vista of the city. The cloud that often shrouds its flat top is known as the Tablecloth, but if the weather's clear, head up for the panorama. At 1,085m, it's a tough trek – go equipped and accompanied, as an urban mountain is no safer than any other. Alternatively, join the (frequently long) queue for the five-minute journey in one of the Swiss-designed cable cars, which began running in 1997 after a third upgrade of the 1929 Aerial Cableway (Tafelberg Road, T 021 424 8181). The cars have revolving floors, affording 360-degree views. There's a self-service café at the summit, but it's better to bring a crisp sauvignon blanc and something delicious from Melissa's (T 021 424 5540) on Kloof Street.

Rhodes Memorial

The wonder of the Sir Herbert Baker and Sir Francis Macey-designed memorial to Cecil John Rhodes, the British diamond magnate, empire builder and Cape Colony prime minister (1890-96), is that no one seems to mind its bombast. Influenced by a Greek temple, it sits, absurdly grandiose amid the wild buck and greenery, on land that was once part of Rhodes' extensive Groote Schuur estate. The rearing horse sculpture celebrates the man's energy, and his bust is at the top of lion-flanked steps, inspired by the Avenue of Sphinxes in Karnak, Egypt. Look out for the remains of his personal zoo. Closed in 1975, infamous escapees included a pair of Himalayan tahrs, which fled into the mountain in the 1930s and prospered. Consider hiking up to the King's Blockhouse, completed in 1796 during the first British occupation.

Disa Park Towers
Unkindly dubbed the Tampon Towers, this trio of 17-storey 1960s apartment blocks is an eyesore to some and an icon to others. Conceived by construction firm Murray & Roberts on the slopes of Table Mountain, their height was controversial, and the summer southeaster, notoriously strong here, exacts its revenge. Shelter at the Deerpark Café (T 021 462 6311).
Chelmsford Road

LANDMARKS

HOTELS
WHERE TO STAY AND WHICH ROOMS TO BOOK

The film and fashion crowds have long had an enduring love affair with photogenic Cape Town, and the accommodation that has sprung up to house them is well equipped to deal with the diva in all of us. Bear in mind that location is important because, although it's not a vast city, Cape Town is divided by its topography. If you're basing yourself on the Atlantic coast, for instance, it's tiresome to keep crossing Kloof Nek to get to the City Bowl. Splitting your stay, with a central stint as well as a beach location, is an ideal solution.

If you're a room-service addict, it's hard to look past the Mount Nelson (76 Orange Street, T 021 483 1000), a grande old dame redesigned by Graham Viney and reinvented as the Claridge's of Cape Town. On the same tip is Cape Grace (West Quay Road, T 021 410 7100), by the V&A Waterfront. Guesthouses and boutique hotels that have a personal touch are flourishing, such as Ellerman House (see p020), 2inn1 Kensington (21 Kensington Crescent, T 021 423 1707), in the residential suburb of Higgovale, and Pod (opposite).

Many of the most interesting places to stay are bijou private rentals. We would recommend Lion's View (see p031), the stylish townhouse rooms of The Village Lodge (49 Napier Street, T 021 421 1106) and the penthouse at Glen Beach Villas (1 Strathmore Road, T 083 675 8266), between Clifton and Camps Bay. There really is no substitute for having your very own Cape Town address.
For full addresses and room rates, see Resources.

Pod

Overlooking Camps Bay's main beach, the rectilinear architecture of Pod is gaining currency along the Atlantic Seaboard. Less clunky than many of the wood-and-steel monstrosities nearby, this svelte 15-room boutique is distinguished by its open-plan interior and thoughtful finishes: marble floors, signature lighting, wooden furniture and a soft winter colour palette. The balconies in the Deluxe Suites (above) allow you to watch the body conscious doing yoga on the beach, or you may prefer the view from the bar/lounge (overleaf). Staying in this part of town does imply an affinity to people traffic, especially in summer, when the restaurants, bars and clubs are jam-packed. Pod's extra-length king-sized beds offer ample reprieve.
3 Argyle Road, T 021 438 8550, www.pod.co.za

Bar/lounge, Pod

HOTELS

Ellerman House & Villa

Once the summer residence of shipping magnate Sir John Ellerman and his wife, this Cape Edwardian mansion has been transformed into the preferred address of visiting film stars and royalty by its art-loving owner, financier Paul Harris. Ellerman House has nine en-suite rooms and two large suites; the styling is a touch old-fashioned so we recommend opting for the neighbouring Ellerman Villa. Here, the Aqua Room (above) has sliding doors leading on to a wood balcony overlooking the ocean. Art is a key part of the decor throughout and there is an excellent gallery (opposite); holdings include works by late-modernist painters Walter Battiss and Douglas Portway, and contemporary pieces by painter/sculptor Mary Sibande, and draughtsman Cameron Platter, son of the wine connoisseur John Platter.
180 Kloof Road, T 021 430 3200, www.ellerman.co.za

021

HOTELS

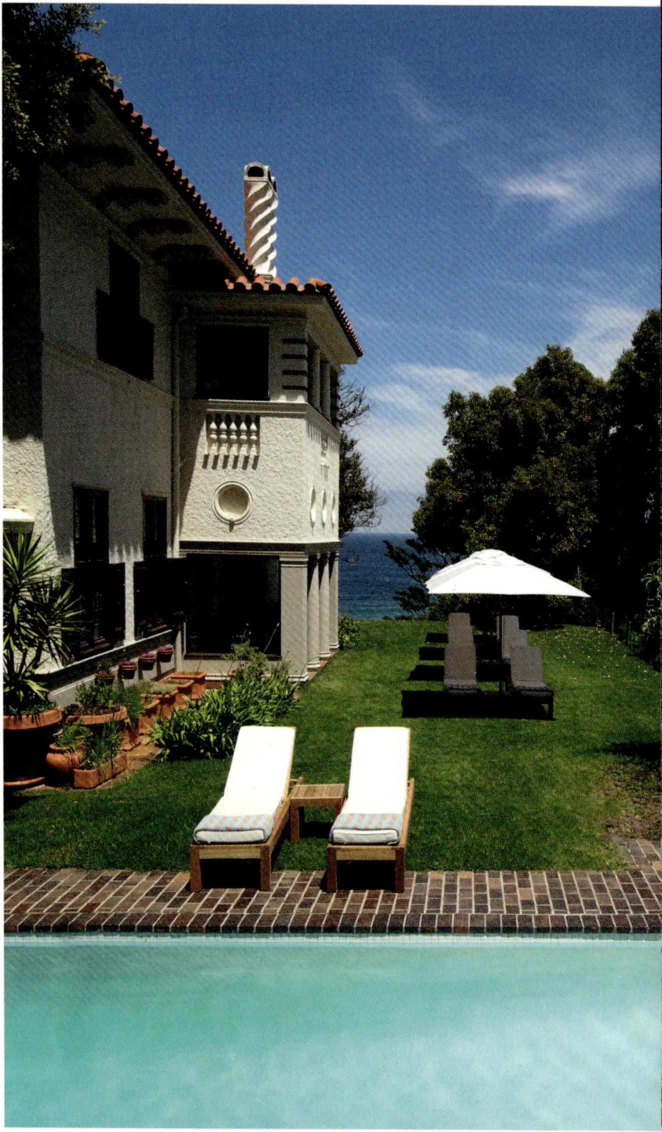

Camps Bay Retreat

Less than a century ago, Camps Bay was a simple getaway for Capetonians on a slow tram, a draw for its breezes and tin beach-huts. That all changed in 1929 when mine owner Friedrich Wilhelm Knacke employed local architect William Grant to design an Edwardian manor house (left) on a bluff between ravines. Now encompassing two adjacent properties, The Villa and Deck House, which feature trim Afro-modern lines, the original property remains the crown jewel here. Its ground- and first-floor suites have classic Cape colonial furnishings; opt for Room One for its four-poster bed, marble art deco bathroom and three balconies, one of which faces Lion's Head. The private reserve has a spa and tennis courts, and a path through stone pines and dramatic scenery leads up to a mountain meditation pool.
7 Chilworth Road, T 021 437 9703, www.campsbayretreat.com

The Grand Daddy

The 1874 building in which The Grand Daddy is housed has been a hotel for more than a century; the elevator in its foyer is one of Cape Town's oldest working lifts. Formerly the Hotel Metropole, it's a popular destination for urbanites aiming to sample Long Street's louche nightlife. We suggest you skip the 23 guest rooms and two suites in favour of one of the seven Airstream trailers on the roof, such as Love of Lace (above) or Pleasantville (opposite), each styled by a local creative. If you're not a guest here, stop for a drink in either the bling Daddy Cool Bar or top-floor Sky Bar. Down the road, former sister hotel Daddy Long Legs (T 021 422 3074) offers 13 individually decorated rooms. In one, The Photo Booth, Antony Smyth's collage of 3,240 black-and-white portraits is an excellent introduction to the locals.
38 Long Street, T 021 424 7247,
www.granddaddy.co.za

HOTELS

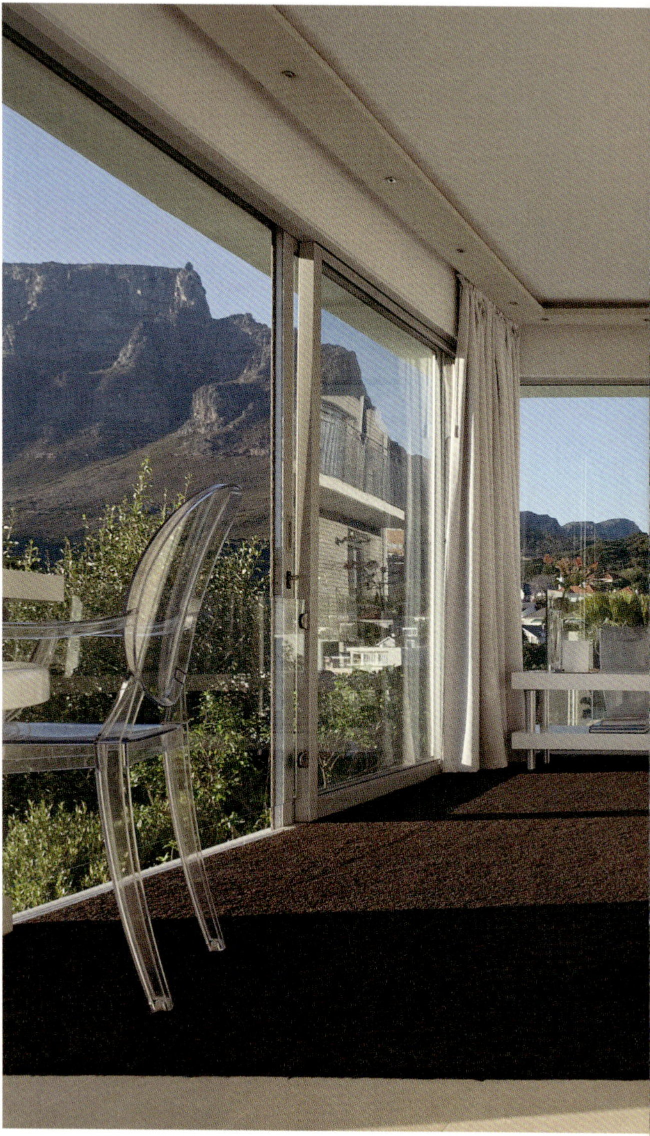

Boutique Manolo
Tucked away in a boho neighbourhood on the slopes of Signal Hill, this modern hotel offers gorgeous views of the City Bowl and Table Mountain. Unassumingly decorated, the property includes a two-storey Penthouse (pictured) with a large terrace, and four smaller suites below that continue the neutral styling.
33 Leeukloof Drive, T 021 426 2330, www.boutique-manolo.co.za

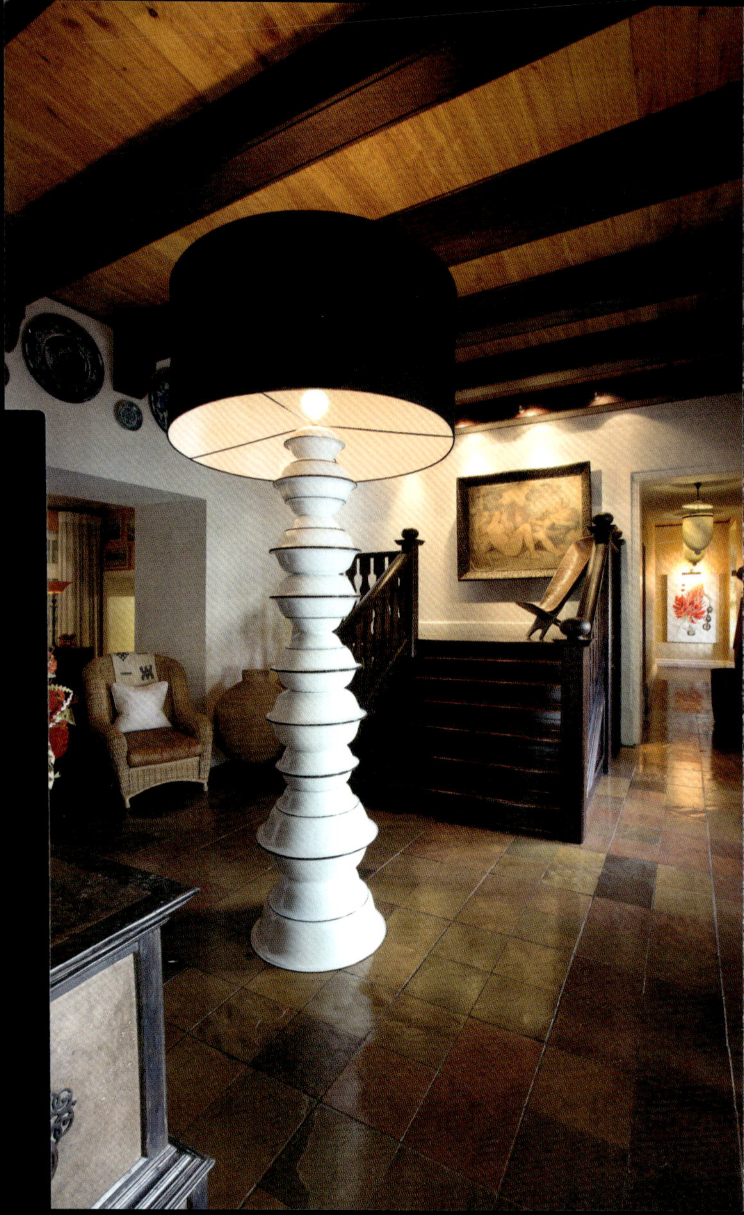

Hout Bay Manor

In 1871, German Jacob Trautmann bought this land from the Kronendal Estate. Built with quarried stone and yellowwood from Hout Bay's once abundant forests, his Royal Hotel became a socialising spot in this outlying Western Cape village. Although still a sleepy hollow, Hout Bay has lost some of its rustic charm due to cheap apartments and unplanned urban sprawl, such as the nearby Imizamo Yethu township. The styling of the hotel, from the foyer (opposite) to the 19 rooms, is informed by Cape Town's multiculturalism, with bright colours, vernacular accents and baroque finishes. We like The Sotho for its garden terrace and alfresco shower, and The Sangoma Suite (above) for its size, free-standing tubs and big balconies.
Baviaanskloof, off Main Road,
T 021 790 0116, www.houtbaymanor.com

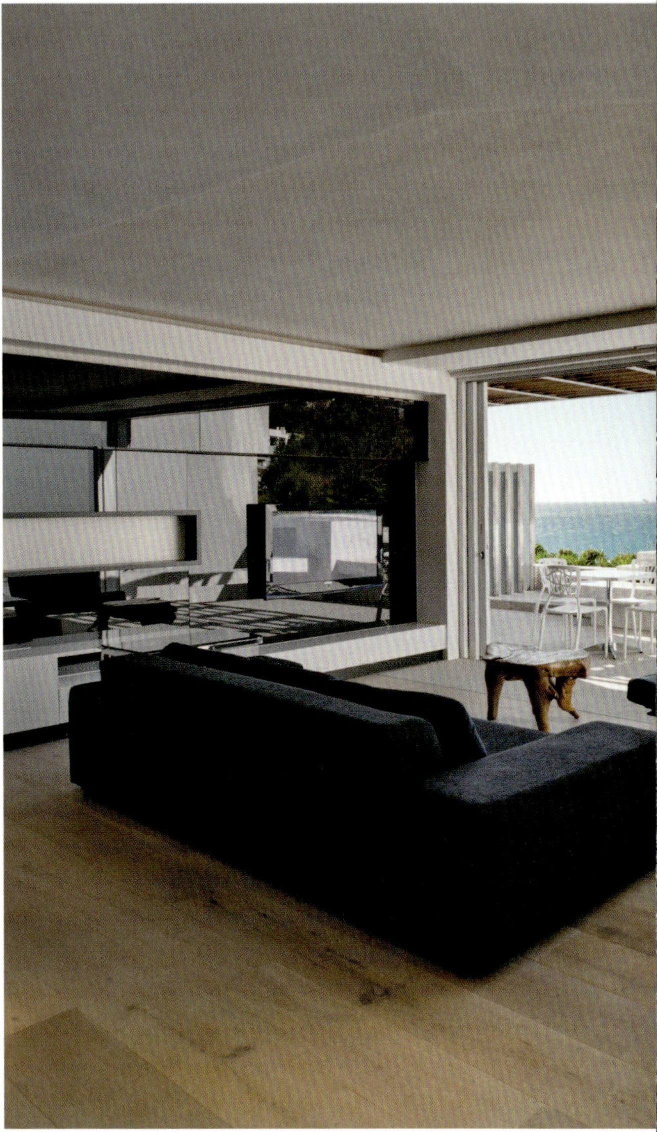

Ebb Tide

This sleek north-facing apartment complex looks towards Lion's Head and Barley Bay, a kink in the Camps Bay coastline celebrated for its irregular right-hand break. Yet you are more likely to spot cyclists than surfers here; riders training for the Cape Argus race pass directly below the outdoor terrace and infinity pool. Designed by Greg Wright, whose geometrically proportioned domestic architecture is redefining the suburb, Ebb Tide is located a short hop to either Beta Beach, in Bakoven, or the bustle of the strip. Comprising four units, of one (left) or three bedrooms, the apartments are distinguished by the use of Volakas marble, a white stone with fine light-grey veins. Wright was also responsible for the equally desirable Lion's View villa and penthouse nearby.
143 Victoria Road, T 083 719 5735, www.ebb-tide.co.za

24 HOURS
SEE THE BEST OF THE CITY IN JUST ONE DAY

Cape Town can please and tease you for a week and still leave you wanting more. But if you have only one day, focus on what the city does best: its culinary delights, nearby winelands, majestic scenery and summer sun on an Atlantic beach. Early risers might consider a pre-breakfast climb up Lion's Head, or a run along Tafelberg Road, at Table Mountain's base; alternatively, Beach Road in Green Point is good for a stroll. We suggest breakfast at Truth (opposite), before enjoying the artworks at Commune1 (see p036). Then head to Woodstock where there is more art at Stevenson (see p038) and delicious lunches at The Kitchen (see p039) and hip Superette (Woodstock Exchange, 66 Albert Road, T 021 802 5525).

There are two main routes to the Cape winelands; if you take the N1, you will pass the Taal Monument (see p040) on the way to Stellenbosch. Of the larger wine estates, Glen Carlou (Simondium Road, Klapmuts, T 021 875 5528), owned by Swiss entrepreneur Donald Hess, displays his modern art collection. On the scenic Helshoogte Pass, Tokara (R310, Stellenbosch, T 021 808 5900) and the nearby Delaire Graff (see p042) offer great views and local art.

In summer, the sun slips over the horizon at about 8pm, which allows you time to stop off at Llandudno beach on your way to Camps Bay for dinner at The Roundhouse (see p056) and revelry at St Yves (see p046). Or head into town to &Union (see p068). *For full addresses, see Resources.*

08.30 Truth Coffee

Cape Town has a surplus of coffee houses; an increasing number of them now do their own roasting. Locals argue whether the best is Origin Coffee at 28 Hudson Street, Deluxe Coffeeworks in Church Street (T 082 681 5740) or Truth.coffeecult, founded by David Donde. Located in a stripped-out warehouse in the East City design precinct, this café and barista school centres on a Victoriana 'steampunk' counter. The space was transformed by Haldane Martin (see p086), whose seating designs are a key element. For breakfast, we like to fuel up with a cup of joe and the 'Johnny Depp' (poached egg and bacon on sourdough with tomato, rocket and hollandaise sauce). Truth has another branch in the Prestwich Memorial in Green Point.
36 Buitenkant Street, T 021 200 0440, www.truthcoffee.com

09.30 Mutual Building
When it was completed in 1940, this 84m, 18-storey art deco masterpiece was hyped as 'the tallest building in Africa – after the pyramids'. As well as the distinctive ziggurat design and triangular windows, look out for the nine sculptural busts and 112.8m-long frieze that envelops three sides of the exterior. It was repurposed into apartments by architects Louis Karol in 2005. The 500 sq m penthouse suite, which is available for short-term rental (T 021 794 3140), has four bedrooms, two of which share a catwalk bridge across the lounge. The main entrance (pictured) features original gold-veined black onyx and gold-leaf detailing. After taking a peek, have a stroll through the bustling Eastern Food Bazaar (T 021 461 2458) nearby at 96 Longmarket Street.
14 Darling Street

24 HOURS

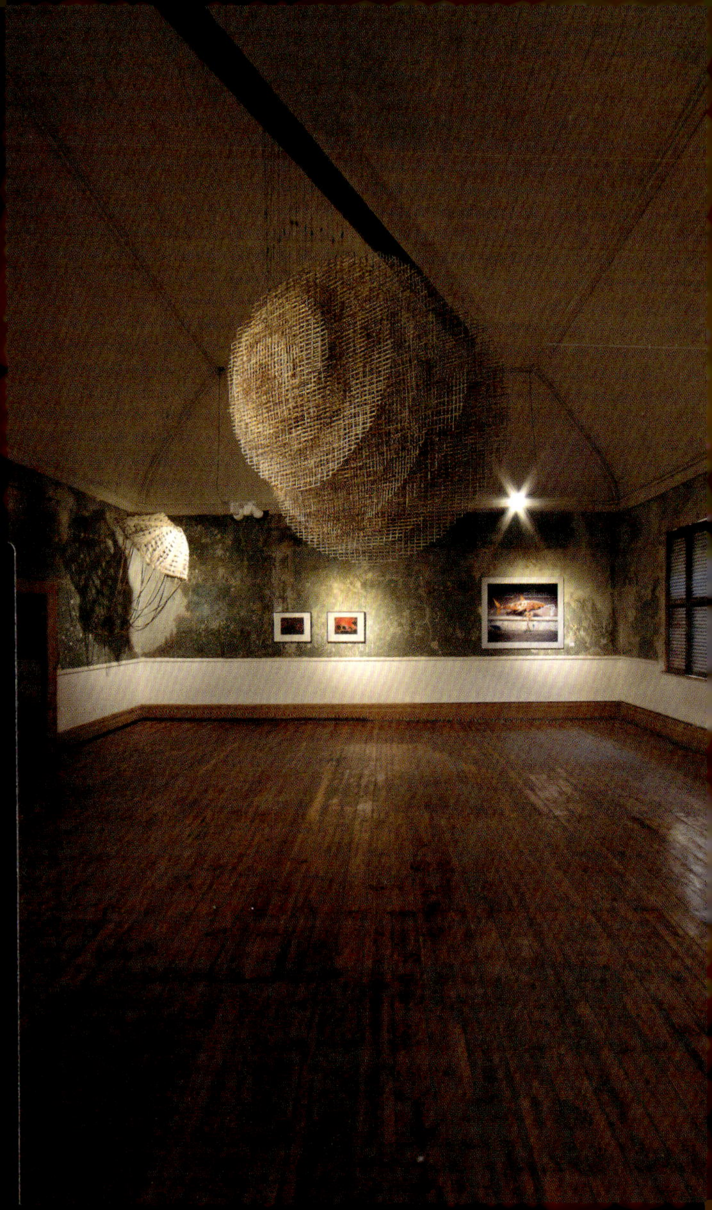

10.00 Commune1

Opened in 2011 by cinematographer and collector Greg Dale, who also restored the venue, Commune1 is a worthy addition to the city's vibrant contemporary art scene. Two big exhibition spaces (one of them double-height with a mezzanine level) and several smaller rooms occupy various historical buildings, including a former funeral home set around a courtyard; the exposed masonry hints at Cape Town's layered architectural styles. Commune1 focuses on experiential work by up-and-coming artists. Past exhibits have included robots playing board games, a tree made out of phone directories, a real-life rainbow and Robyn Farah's *Belloons* (above). 'Salvo' (opposite) featured work by Christopher Swift, Natasha Norman and Gordon Clark. *64 Wale Street, T 021 423 5600, www.commune1.com*

11.30 Stevenson

Sir Lowry Road cuts through the centre of Woodstock and is home to two of South Africa's leading contemporary art galleries, this one and Goodman Gallery (T 021 462 7573), which pioneered the market here. Both inhabit intelligently conceived spaces. Stevenson's street-level venue is museum-like in scale, its restrained white interior-layout the work of Johannesburg designer Lunetta Bartz. Stevenson is strong on photography, having showcased the likes of Guy Tillim, Zanele Muholi, Pieter Hugo and Viviane Sassen (*Parasomnia*, above), and painting (Penny Siopis, Deborah Poynton, Zander Blom). Ask to see the portfolio of Serge Alain Nitegeka, the gallery's young Burundian sculptor whose work has a distinctive modern aesthetic.
Buchanan Building, 160 Sir Lowry Road, T 021 462 1500, www.michaelstevenson.com

12.15 The Kitchen
By the time *The New York Times* profiled Karen Dudley's café, the secret was out, her lunchtime venue packed with ad execs, hipsters and ladies from the nicer suburbs. Initially trading from the Neighbourgoods Market (see p080), Dudley opened her eaterie in 2009 to coincide with a wave of galleries moving to Woodstock; it also allowed her to consolidate her catering business. Decorated with antique crockery and culinary oddities, The Kitchen's menu includes chef Dudley's legendary gourmet sandwiches (including honey mustard sausage and aubergine with Danish feta), salads and sweet nibbles. Try the bulgar wheat with roasted peppers, dates and coriander, or the delectable ginger fudge squares – they're small and guilt-free.
111 Sir Lowry Road, T 021 462 2201, www.karendudley.co.za

14.00 Taal Monument
Architect Jan van Wijk's remarkable 1974 tribute to Afrikaans, South Africa's unique hybrid language, is, if nothing else, a great picnic spot on the way to the winelands of Franschhoek (see p100) and Stellenbosch. Afrikaans is the third most widely spoken of the country's 11 official languages, after Zulu and Xhosa. It is a mixture of Dutch (mainly), French, English, Malay, German and indigenous tongues, all of which are symbolically recognised in these granite columns. When the Taal Monument was built, Afrikaans was heavily associated with apartheid; the government policy of making it the only language of instruction in schools led to the Soweto uprising of 1976. In Cape Town alone, 92 people were killed as a result. Afrikaans, though, is still vibrant and is the lingua franca beyond most of metropolitan South Africa.
Gabbema Doordrift Street, Paarl Mountain, T 021 872 3441, www.taalmuseum.co.za

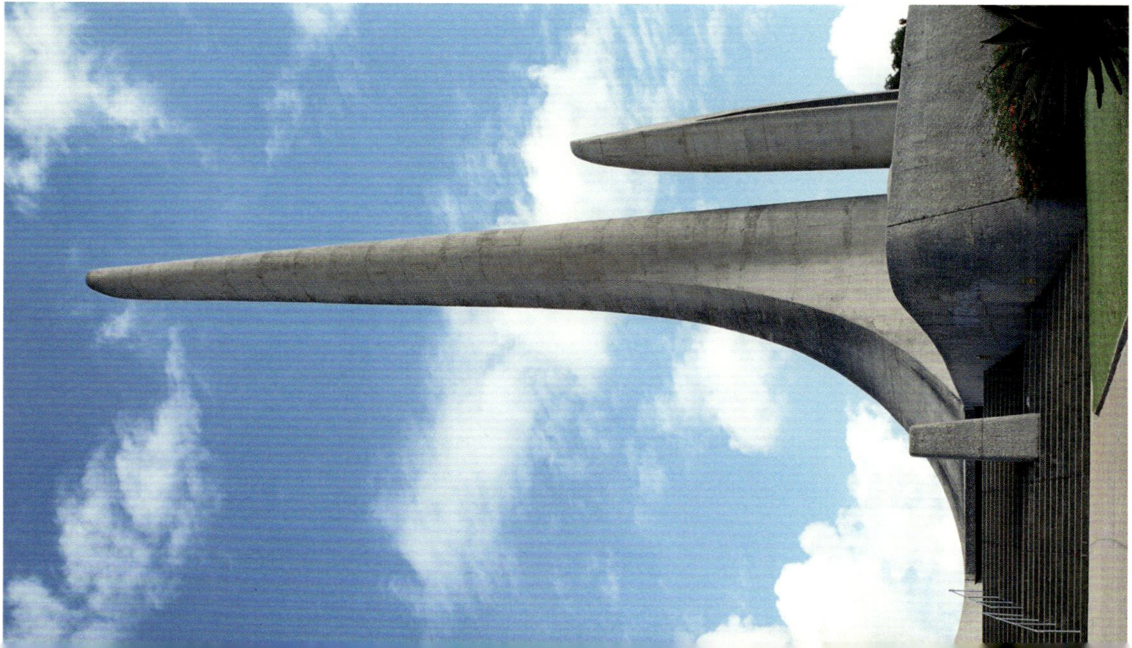

14.30 Delaire Graff Estate

Owned by the diamond and gem dealer Laurence Graff, this winery reopened in 2009 after a rebuild by architect Derek Henstra, whose previous projects include Mandela Rhodes Place in Cape Town. Situated on a rise looking out towards the Simonsberg and Drakenstein mountains, the main building is bisected by a stone spine wall that runs the length of the site, parallel to a row of pin oak trees outside.

There is a tasting lounge (above) and also a restaurant, Indochine, with interiors by David Collins that feature handblown glass lighting and marble fireplaces. The spa offers private suites and has a 22m infinity pool. Graff is a major art collector and selected many of the pieces that are displayed throughout the estate.
R130, Helshoogte Pass, Stellenbosch, T 021 885 8160, www.delaire.co.za

16.30 Honest

Established by Anthony Gird and Michael de Klerk, this artisanal company makes delicious treats using organic cacao. The key ingredient is ethically sourced from Ecuador before being transformed here into bonbon truffles, bottled spreads and divinely packaged slabs. The latter make great gifts as the eight wrappers have been designed by local artists; Kalahari Desert Salt features work by illustrator Toby Newsome and the 88 per cent dark option showcases painter Michael Taylor. The glass-fronted shop is immediately identifiable by its distinctive gold lettering, which recalls an older, more Victorian Cape Town. Interiors include traditional leather weave seating, which is known as *riem stoels*. Closes at 2pm on Saturdays. *66 Wale Street, T 021 423 8762, www.honestchocolate.co.za*

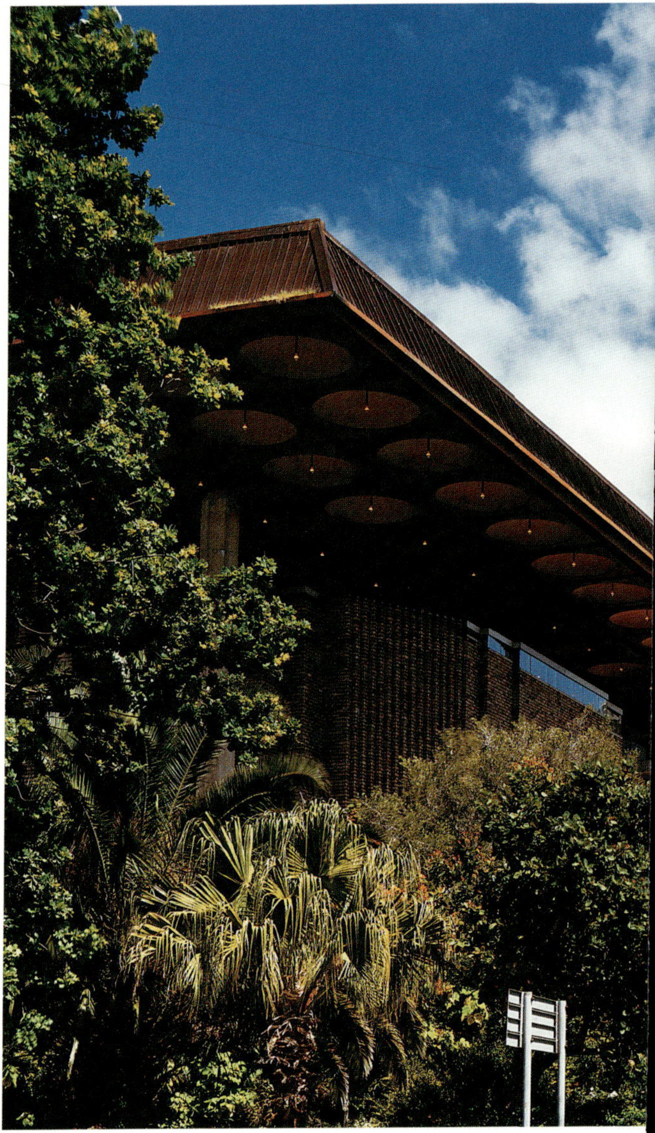

19.30 Baxter Theatre Centre
Among the city's notable theatres are the acclaimed Fugard (T 021 461 4554) and this 1977 brick masterpiece by Jack Barnett. Also comprising a concert hall, it was open to all during segregation. The imposing exterior has some intricate touches, and the recessed orange dome lights above the entrance are a taste of dozens more that line the ceiling inside.
Main Road, Rondebosch, T 021 685 7880

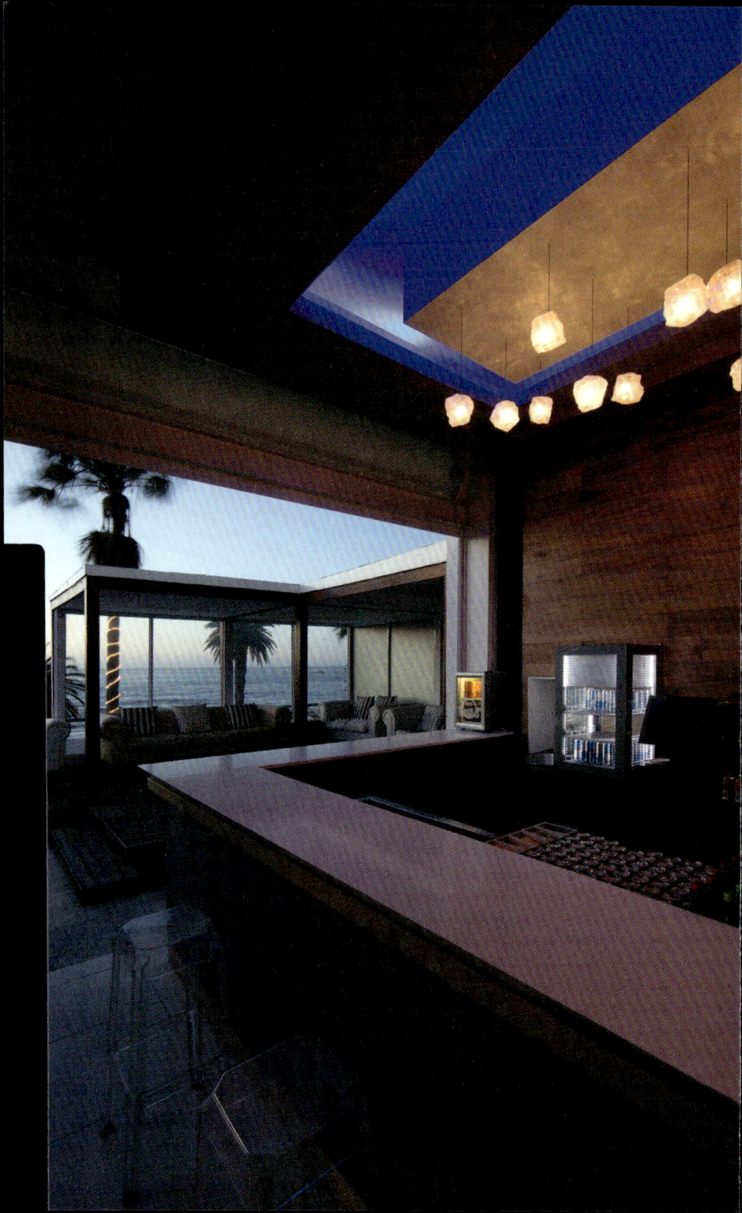

22.00 St Yves Beach Club
Cape Town after dark has its designated party haunts: hipsters prefer the City Bowl, the V&A Waterfront is for people in socks and sandals, and Camps Bay has long been the place where the beautiful set stay up late. Café Caprice (T 021 438 8315) on Victoria Road is an institution, but its street location can be annoying in summer when the pavements become congested with musclemen and scammers. Tactfully set above the hubbub, overlooking the main beach, St Yves was redesigned by Gregor Breber of local partnership Soda Stream. Take in the expansive sunset from the outdoor lounging area (above), with its Riviera-style daybeds, before heading indoors. The venue hosts a reliable line-up of top DJs spinning blissful beats.
The Promenade, Victoria Road,
T 021 438 0826, www.styves.co.za

URBAN LIFE
CAFÉS, RESTAURANTS, BARS AND NIGHTCLUBS

It took a while, but in 2006 two South African restaurants were, for the first time, listed among the world's best places to eat. Both are in Cape Town and French-influenced: La Colombe (Spaanschemat River Road, T 021 794 2390) in Constantia, and Le Quartier Français (16 Huguenot Road, T 021 876 2151) in Franschhoek, have lent credibility to the city's deserved reputation as a foodies' paradise. Although prices and service can sometimes raise an eyebrow, the overall quality of food will satisfy even the fussiest epicurean.

Restaurants in beachside areas can get sloppy in high season, but the City Bowl eateries are dependable, and the cafés in outer suburbs such as Muizenberg and Kalk Bay are a revelation. Many wineries have great restaurants as well as tasting rooms, such as Indochine in Delaire Graff (see p042) and the standalone delights of Reuben's (19 Huguenot Road, T 021 876 3772) in Franschhoek.

The turnover of establishments tends to be high; venues can be the in-thing for six months and then disappear off the radar. But you can't go wrong with long-term favourites such as La Perla (Beach Road, T 021 439 9538), decorated with paintings from SMAC Art Gallery (In-Fin Art Building, Buitengracht Street/Buitensingel Street, T 021 422 5100). More recent arrivals, such as Carne SA (see p054), and the art-strewn 6 Spin Street (see p067), in a sensitively restored 1902 Sir Herbert Baker building, could well be here to stay. *For full addresses, see Resources.*

Hemelhuijs

The sans serif signage of Jacques Erasmus' bistro, launched in 2010, hints at what to expect inside: unembellished luxury. The trim modernist tables and chairs were custom-made and complement the sleek shelving, some of which is used to showcase Hemelhuijs' range of Asian-inspired home furnishings. According to Erasmus, a restaurant and food consultant, the sepia tableware is not only covetable but retains heat for longer. The design philosophy is wabi-sabi, offset by decadent displays of flowers and objets trouvés. The seasonal menu has some excellent staples, such as *frikkadel* (meatballs) served with buttery mash, and trout with pomegranate and herb remoulade. Wash it down with the house label shiraz or sauvignon blanc.
71 Waterkant Street, T 021 418 2042, www.hemelhuijs.co.za

The Power & The Glory
Seen at night from the busy intersection where this split-level café and bar is found, it has the look of a disreputable watering hole for artists and hipsters. But arrive before The Black Ram bar opens at 5pm, and the laidback ambience is as surprising as the cappuccinos in Le Creuset crockery and the organic-themed menu. The salty pretzel hot dog is an institution.
13d Kloof Nek Road, T 021 422 2108

URBAN LIFE

Manna Epicure
Situated at the upper end of Kloof Street, away from the hustle, Manna Epicure is a draw for its daytime menu, all-white decor and funky organic chandeliers. Launched in 2005 by the dream team of Maranda Engelbrecht — now at Babylonstoren (see p097) — and Jacques Erasmus, who currently runs Hemelhuijs (see p049), Manna Epicure's quirky dishes blend sweet and savoury in tasty combinations. Watermelon and basil with Danish feta, roasted pumpkin seeds and serrano ham is a great lunch choice, but we suggest you come here to start your day; try the renowned homemade coconut bread, with eggs, smoked salmon and avocado. Aim for a seat on the shaded terrace with the well-heeled City Bowl socialites, many of whom turn breakfast into lunch.
151 Kloof Street, T 021 426 2413

The Greenhouse
The pitch is simple: a fine-dining restaurant in a superlative Constantia Valley property within a conservatory on the forested slopes of Table Mountain. Proving equal to the Edenic setting, chef Peter Tempelhoff has crafted a menu that showcases his masterful use of local ingredients. Peaks include quail and sultana-glazed pork belly, and Outeniqua springbok loin with purple figs and foie gras. The three eating areas are cleverly linked by local designers Dawn Dickerson and Carmel Naudé of HotCocoa, using simple elements such as standing lamps, leafy motifs and floral wallpaper. The preferred tables are in architect David Misplon's gorgeous glass box (above). Booking is essential.
The Cellars-Hohenort,
93 Brommersvlei Road, T 021 794 2137,
www.cellars-hohenort.com

Carne SA

When gregarious restaurateur Giorgio Nava opened 95 Keerom (T 021 422 0765) in the former stables and slave quarters of Company's Garden, many were seduced by the pared-down excellence of his food. Nava is a proponent of modern Italian cooking with a Milanese accent. South Africans, though, are avid red-meat eaters, which accounts for Nava's second venture, dedicated entirely to matters of the flesh.

Offering fine cuts of Romagnola beef, Dorper lamb and game, Carne SA's menu includes grass-fed calves' liver, seared rib-eye scaloppini and lamb shoulder stuffed with spinach, sultanas and pine nuts. The dark, masculine interior of this split-level venue is inspired by an Italian butchers and is as unfussy as 95 Keerom.
70 Keerom Street, T 021 424 3460, www.carne-sa.com

URBAN LIFE

The Roundhouse
This fine-dining institution, situated on the slopes of Lion's Head overlooking the Twelve Apostles, is housed in a 1786 building that was formerly a hotel, tea-room and Lord Charles Somerset's hunting lodge. Chef Eric Bulpitt has worked at The Ledbury in London and Noma in Copenhagen; his menu includes fallow deer loin and west coast mussels.
Kloof Road, The Glen, T 021 438 4347

URBAN LIFE

Grand Café & Beach

It's amazing what a few truckloads of imported white sand can do. Set on a small harbour adjacent to the V&A Waterfront, this artificial-beach café/dinner venue has taken a perennial theme – bohemian baroque – and run with it. The main dining hall is in a former boathouse decorated with huge chandeliers, French bistro chairs and antique Indian rugs, whereas outside it's a choice between terrace seating or loafing on loungers. The Grand is a lifestyle pitch, hence the well-stocked retail boutique. It attracts quite a scene at sundown so be sure to book ahead; alternatively try its sister venue (T 021 438 4253) on the promenade in Camps Bay. The simple menu focuses on favourites such as line-caught fish.
Granger Bay Road, off Beach Road, T 021 425 0551, www.grandafrica.com

Clarke's Bar & Dining Room

In 2011, Lyndall Maunder left Superette (see p032) and opened this no-frills diner. A simple metal counter and pendant lighting underscore the venue's utilitarian approach to decor (and menu design) but the mood is softened by the shelves laden with terracotta pot plants. In summer, the pavement pine deck, with its benches, planters and bike parking bays, is ideal for watching the foot traffic. Many eateries are competing for the title of the city's top burger joint, but Clarke's legendary cheese patty certainly ranks among the best. The free-range beef, courtesy of Bill Riley Meat, comes in an artisan bun from baker Trevor Daly. The drinks menu includes local beers such as Jack Black, Birkenhead and Darling Brew's Native Ale. *133 Bree Street, T 021 424 7648, www.clarkesdining.co.za*

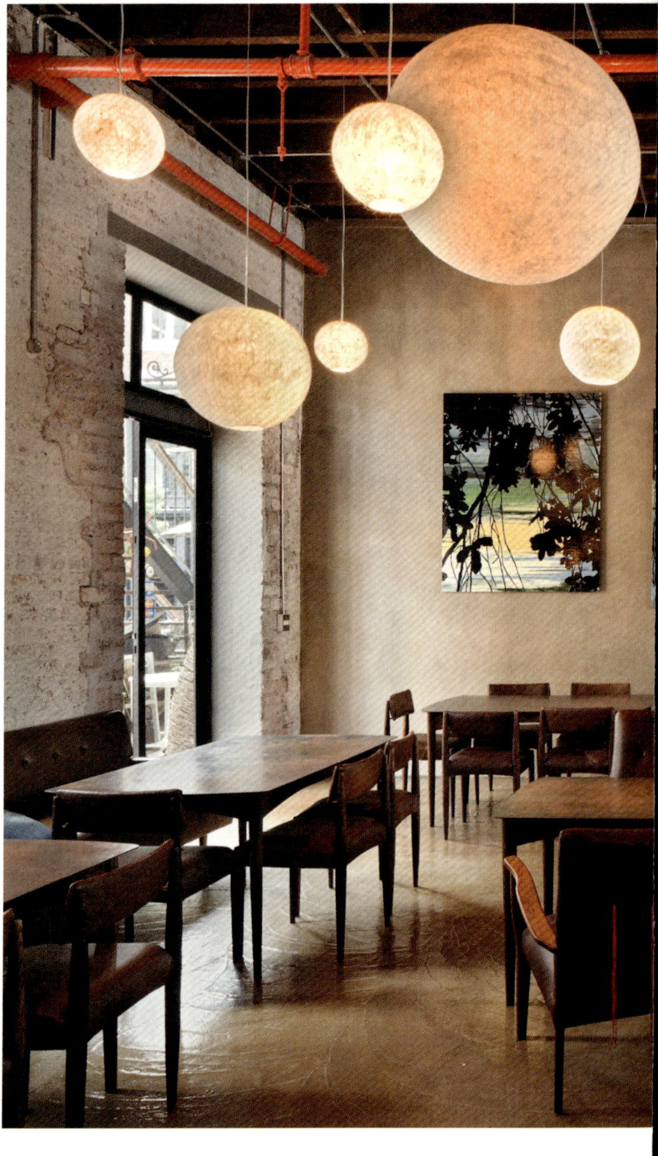

Test Kitchen
Chef Luke Dale-Roberts made his name at the superb La Colombe (see p048) and founded the 30-seat Test Kitchen in order to experiment. There are casual and formal menu options, featuring dishes such as pan-seared duck, sake-steamed foie gras, kumquats and turnip purée. Open Tuesdays to Saturdays.
Shop 104a, The Old Biscuit Mill, 375 Albert Road, T 021 447 2337

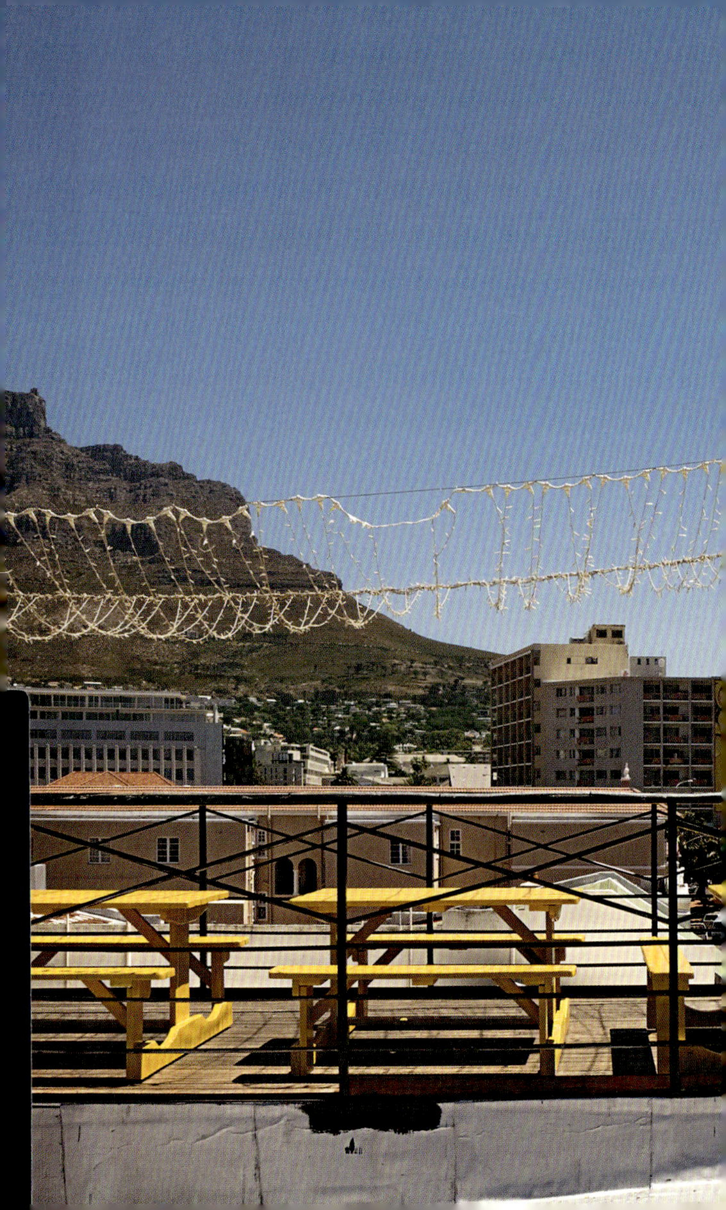

Royale Eatery

Tucked unobtrusively among the raft of wannabe NYC East Village bars and eateries on Long Street, this burger joint/diner has spawned a mini-empire that now sprawls across three floors. As soon as you tuck into one of the juicy patties, which range from the orthodox to the ethical (vegetarian options are plentiful) and exotic (ostrich with beetroot relish), you will understand why this venue is consistently packed. If it's full, leave your name at the counter and climb a perilous flight of stairs to the shabby-chic bar, The Waiting Room, where we suggest you try a Laurentina beer from Mozambique. If the band or the DJ soundtrack gets too loud, head to the roof terrace (opposite), which has panoramic views. Closed Sundays.
273 Long Street, T 021 422 4536, www.royaleeatery.com

The Woodlands Eatery
A boho bistro in a shopping mall opposite a school, in an area known for gale-force winds, sounds like an unlikely recipe for success. Yet co-owner Larry Steenkamp's gourmet pizzas (try the lamb), steak and seafood dishes have beaten the odds. The objets d'art and vintage finds that abound are key to the congenial and unfussy vibe. Closed Mondays.
2 Deerpark Drive West, T 021 801 5799

URBAN LIFE

Harbour House

This glass-box seafood restaurant would be a tourist trap anywhere else, but here, built on a breakwater in Kalk Bay, it works as a modest temple to simply prepared fish in a low-key, amicable setting. The cuisine is international with Mediterranean influences and much of the day's catch comes from the restaurant's own boat. We recommend the west coast mussels and the house fish soup. If all the tables are taken, have a drink on the sofas on the terrace and watch the goings-on in the harbour. The restaurant overlooks False Bay, and from July until November you may spot southern right whales as they come inshore to calf. Downstairs, The Polana (T 021 788 7162) serves delicious slabs of meat as well as seafood.
First floor, Kalk Bay Harbour,
T 021 788 4133, www.harbourhouse.co.za

6 Spin Street

Many of Sir Herbert Baker's signature SA buildings are located in Johannesburg and Pretoria, but here he designed Wynberg Boys' High School, St George's Anglican Cathedral and 6 Spin Street. The venue reopened in 2010 as a conference centre, bookstore and restaurant. Wooden doors open on to the main dining room, which has large arched windows, a fireplace and a ceiling mobile by Brendhan Dickerson and Petra Keinhorst (*In The Balance*, above). There's also a sculpture, by Ed Young, of Desmond Tutu swinging from a chandelier. The venue is the brainchild of art-lover Robert Mulders, whose Rozenhof was cherished by foodies. Every fortnight the menu includes a dish made using a recipe from one of the old-fashioned cookbooks.
6 Spin Street, T 021 461 0666, www.6spinstreet.co.za

&Union

Opened by Rui Esteves and Brad Armitage, who founded the Vida e Caffè brand, this self-styled beer salon and charcuterie is a popular evening hangout. As with many venues around Heritage Square, the listed architecture required compromise: the tiled inner bar area has low wood ceilings that make it feel a tad cramped, so many patrons prefer to sit outside, where singer-songwriters provide accompaniment; during the wet winter months, the party continues under a Moroccan-style tent. The house beers, now widely distributed, are brewed in Bavaria and Belgium, and won't disappoint. Try the Berne Unfiltered Amber, a buttery brew, or the malty Dark Lager, its colour matching the bar's chocolate interiors. Closed Sundays and Mondays.
110 Bree Street, T 021 422 2770,
www.andunion.com

URBAN LIFE

INSIDER'S GUIDE
LIAM MOONEY, INTERIOR DESIGNER

Much of Liam Mooney's routine happens within walking distance of his townhouse, in the relaxed City Bowl suburb of Gardens, and his showroom (64 Wale Street, T 770 7461), in the CBD. He often starts the day with brunch at Clarke's (see p059) or coffee at Haas (see p087). When he has some free time, he drops into menswear designer Adriaan Kuiters (73 Kloof Street, T 021 424 5502), or Chandler House (53 Church Street, T 083 423 2001), a modern design boutique that has roots in the Arts and Crafts movement. Mooney is also a fan of the city's informal retail, notably the Earth Fair Food Market (St George's Mall; Thursday 11am-3pm) and Milnerton Flea Market (Paarden Eiland, T 021 551 7879; Sunday). 'I once found a Parker Knoll armchair there for R400,' he says.

On wind-free summer afternoons, he heads out to Beta Beach in Bakoven. 'It's small, secluded and has great rocks for jumping into the ocean.' Or if he's feeling lazy, Mooney may take his trunks to Sky Bar (49 Napier Street, T 021 421 1106), a rooftop pool and lounge. He often dines at classic bistro The Duchess of Wisbeach (3 Wisbeach Road, T 021 434 1525) or Mano's (39 Main Road, T 021 434 1090), a 'super relaxed' European-style eaterie. For an upbeat night out, he likes &Union (see p068) for its live music and craft beer, and PISCO Bar (50 Waterkant Street, T 021 419 2633), a Peruvian tapas joint with a dancey after-hours scene.

For full addresses, see Resources.

URBAN LIFE

ARCHITOUR
A GUIDE TO CAPE TOWN'S ICONIC BUILDINGS

In 2011, Cape Town beat Bilbao and Dublin to the title of World Design Capital 2014. The accolade is perhaps deceptive – the city possesses few signature public buildings, certainly nothing to rival Frank Gehry's Guggenheim Museum. The centre is littered with apartheid-era state-sponsored architecture, like Customs House (Heerengracht Street), which is a robust example of 1960s SA modernism. The Civic Centre (see p076) replaced the imperial-style City Hall (Darling Street, T 021 465 2029), which dates from 1905 and is now a cultural space. And the 1950s Railway Station (Adderley Street) has also had a makeover, by architect Mokena Makeka. Yet the most fascinating projects today are less about statement-making and more about a cleverly designed township school or arts centre, for instance Makeka Design Lab's Railway Police Station (Zwaans Road) in Retreat, or Noero Wolff Architects' Usasazo Secondary School (7778 Bangiso Drive) in Khayelitsha.

Alternatively, Higgovale is home to some audacious domestic architecture, and modernist homes decorate the slopes of Camps Bay and Clifton – Stefan Antoni's consummate Villa St Leon (3a St Leon Avenue, T 021 434 6158) can be rented. The wineries that have sprung up amid Stellenbosch's gabled vernacular are as enticing for their design as their grapes; the 2004 Waterkloof (Sir Lowry's Pass Road, Somerset West, T 021 858 1292) gleefully flouts tradition. *For full addresses, see Resources.*

Ritz Hotel

A jaded 1970s tower with what looks like a spaceship on top, this is the least ritzy Ritz you are likely to find. The hotel has been unkindly nicknamed the Pitz, but we don't feel the structure itself should take the blame for that. Lurking off Main Road in Sea Point, it rises, almost embarrassed, above the rows of Victorian, Edwardian and modernist houses, and is far and away the most interesting building in the area. The spaceship section is actually the revolving Top of the Ritz restaurant (T 021 439 6988) on the 21st storey. The bar is on the same floor but, somewhat thoughtlessly, not in the bit that goes round. So, to take a spin, you will have to order a prawn cocktail, which should nicely complete the whole time-warp experience.

Main Road/Camberwell Road, T 021 439 6010, www.cape-town-ritz-hotel.com

The Spa House
Cape Town's contemporary residential architecture is superlative – there's a surfeit of talent, space and cash to play with here. A prime example is the linear form and imaginative rationalism of this Hout Bay retreat, by Metropolis Design's Jon Jacobson. The living quarters appear to float and the spa is submerged into the pool. Better yet, you can rent it out.
Avenue Suzanne, T 021 790 8737

075

ARCHITOUR

Civic Centre
Naudé, Papendorf, Van der Merwe and Meiring's 1979 Civic Centre – a brutalist concrete-and-glass tower, 98m tall and twice as long, with a lower podium building in front of it – wasn't the most obvious choice for the home of Cape Town's newly unified city government (Unicity) in late 2000. But the podium was expertly renovated by architects KrugerRoos, who added an upper level to create a structure that is all about openness and light, with glass used wherever possible to underline the transparency of civic business. The inverted steel cone that forms the roof of the council chamber (right) symbolises a fresh start, and is a wind disperser and shading device. It also contributes to the acoustics and changes colour with the weather. It is not, as some locals first thought, scaffolding that got left behind.
12 Hertzog Boulevard, T 021 400 2303

ARCHITOUR

Guga S'Thebe Arts & Culture Centre
Winner of the 2008 Global Award for Sustainable Architecture, Carin Smuts constructs low-cost public buildings in consultation with the communities they serve. She was the lead designer of this mixed-use cultural centre, which opened in 1999 in Langa, the city's oldest township (established in 1923). It is intended to resemble a traditional settlement – the golden cone is a contemporary take on the circular hut. Local artists and children created murals for the exterior walls. When Smuts carried her distinctive aesthetic to her Sea Point studio (T 021 433 1330), outraged neighbours spray-painted her wall. Smuts' retort: she framed the graffiti. You can visit Guga S'Thebe independently or as part of a half-day township tour of Langa with Cape Capers (T 021 448 3117).
Washington Street, Langa, T 021 695 3493

ARCHITOUR

SHOPPING
THE BEST RETAIL THERAPY AND WHAT TO BUY

Kloof Street's tony boutiques and De Waterkant's trendy interiors stores are moochers' paradises, full of charming one-offs. Plenty of retailers stock the work of local designers, whose individual studios can often be visited if you wish to place a commission. Some are in the CBD, like Heather Moore's Skinny LaMinx (201 Bree Street, T 021 424 6290), but the majority are in Woodstock, including bespoke lightmaker Heath Nash (2 Mountain Road, T 021 447 5757), design boutique Casamento (160 Albert Road, T 021 448 6183) and furniture guru Haldane Martin (see p086). Likened to lower Manhattan pre-gentrification, the area is home to The Old Biscuit Mill (375 Albert Road, T 021 486 5999), which hosts the lively Neighbourgoods Market on Saturdays, and The Woodstock Exchange (66-68 Albert Road, T 021 486 5999), where you'll find the minimal homewares of Pedersen + Lennard (T 021 447 2020).

Crafts are a good buy here. African Image (Burg Street/Church Street, T 021 423 8385) is popular, but Africa Nova (72 Waterkant Street, T 021 425 5123) is our tip for handwoven Kente cloth and Astrid Dahl's organic ceramics; and Missibaba (229 Bree Street, T 021 424 8127) sells fine leather goods. Also spearheading the CBD revival is Klûk (47 Bree Street, T 083 377 7780), which stocks South African couture. Edgier fashion is found where Church and Long Street meet, notably at MeMeMe (117a Long Street, T 021 424 0001). *For full addresses, see Resources.*

Frazer Parfum

Following in the family footsteps, Tammy Frazer, the granddaughter of Graham Wulff, the chemist who invented Oil of Olay, established this small, bespoke perfume house in 2008. Her brand has fostered a strong international reputation through a commitment to natural and organic raw materials that are sourced direct from growers. Frazer's palette incorporates rare absolutes, concretes and resins coupled with chemotyped essential oils, petals, woods, roots, grass and zest. The ready-to-wear collection, Chapters, is on sale locally at Merchants On Long (see p084). The perfume is beautifully decanted into a *flacon* (above), handblown by glass artist David Reade. Frazer also creates made-to-order scents.
108 Bree Street (by appointment only), T 082 463 5104, www.frazerparfum.com

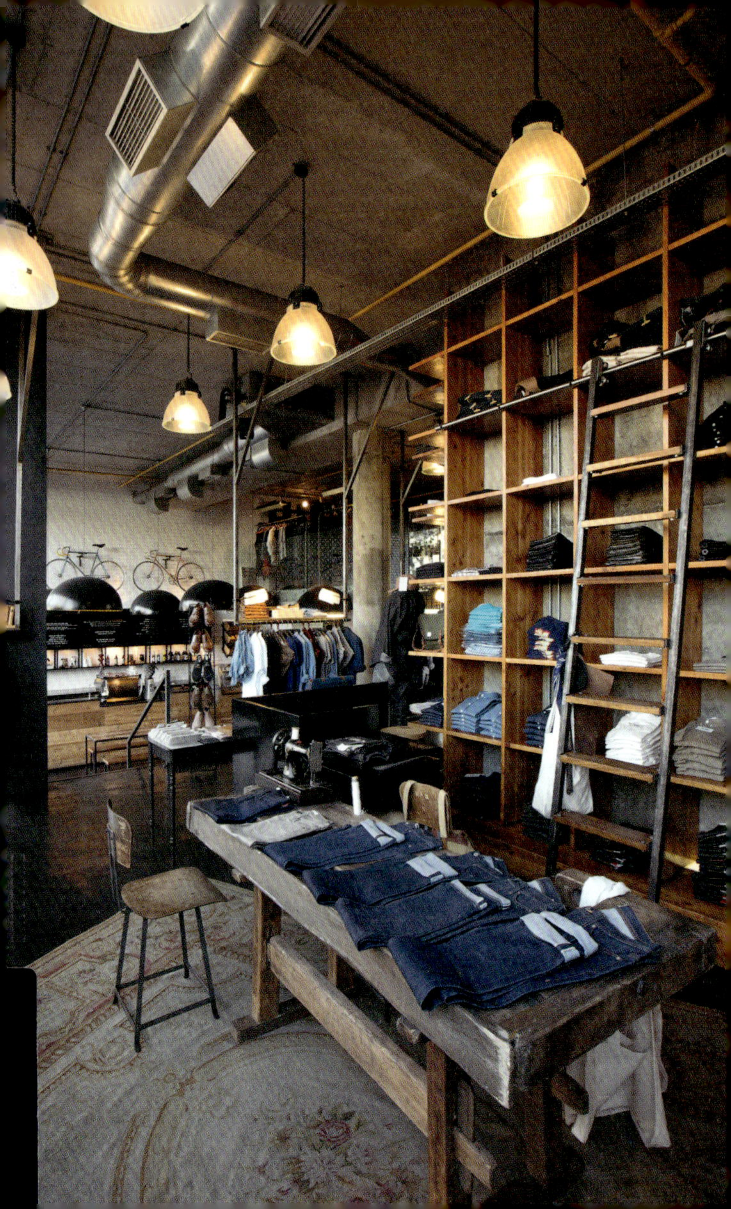

Loading Bay
Although Cape Town likes to foreground its European heritage, it often shares more of a kinship with West Coast USA, especially in its brashness – this extends to its fashion sensibilities. Similar in outlook to LA's Fred Segal, Loading Bay makes a bold stand for better male grooming. The essence of the collection of dapper brands here, among them Acne, APC and Velour, is tailored simplicity; this in a city that still venerates surf baggies. The imported labels are the main draw, and it's a favourite destination of designer Liam Mooney (see p070). But the split-level brick-and-glass venue in a former De Waterkant warehouse is also popular for its café (above, T 021 425 6321), which serves breakfast and lunch using ingredients sourced from local farmers.
30 Hudson Street, T 021 425 6320, www.loadingbay.co.za

Merchants On Long

This concept retail emporium owned by Hanneli Rupert – a scion of the Rupert dynasty – is a treasure trove of African fashion and accessories. Formerly a Greco-Roman-inspired bathhouse (circa 1890), it still boasts an art nouveau terracotta facade that was imported from Edinburgh and re-erected in 1903. When the previous tenant moved out, the interior cladding was stripped to expose Table Mountain slate and original timber beams. Wares include Zimbabwean jewellery by Patrick Mavros, South African ceramics, handmade clothing from Kenya, and Rupert's own luxury leather purses. Merchants also facilitates collaborations between local designers to create exclusive in-house lines.
34 Long Street, T 021 422 2828, www.merchantsonlong.com

SHOPPING

Haldane Martin

When Haldane Martin moved from his old premises, a former church, into this retail space on Sir Lowry Road, he created a taut lattice of yellow rope as a partition wall that intrigued passersby. The attention proved a shot of adrenalin for the designer, known for his 'Shongololo' chair (above, centre), prompting innovative displays using the rope as a backdrop. Martin came to prominence with his egg-shaped 'Zulu Mama' chair, which utilises indigenous weaving techniques. His 'Source' range updates this with wire mesh, inspired by the growth patterns of leaves and petals. Martin mostly works in metal but used wood, and pink caning made by local artisans, for his 'Riempie' chairs, a funky update of classic Cape furniture.
Fairweather House, 176 Sir Lowry Road, T 021 461 1785, www.haldanemartin.co.za

Haas Collective

A big draw in the friendlier lower part of Bo-Kaap – a Malay community on the edge of the CBD known for its vibrantly coloured homesteads – the Haas Collective pulls together an intriguing boutique store, a design gallery and a coffee house with its own roastery. Set across two buildings, the businesses tend to overlap, with flat-white-sipping patrons seated among items for sale. These range from gifts, including ceramic sculptures by Rebecca Townsend and jewellery from the Francois Irvine studio, to larger singular works, such as the repurposed baroque furniture and taxidermied birds and deer. It's frivolously OTT – the staff even dress in top hats.
67 Rose Street, T 021 422 4413,
www.haascollective.com

SPORTS AND SPAS
WORK OUT, CHILL OUT OR JUST WATCH

There is much to please thrill-seekers in this city. The mountains, apart from being good to climb (Mountain Club of South Africa, T 021 465 3412), can be fun to leap off too. You might want to abseil (Abseil Africa, T 021 424 4760) down Table Mountain or paraglide (Cape Town Tandem Paragliding, T 076 892 2283) from Lion's Head. Mountain biking (Downhill Adventures, T 021 422 0388) is also popular. At sea level, take a ride on a 58ft schooner (Waterfront Boat Company, T 021 418 5806) or try kayaking (PaddleYak, T 044 533 0537), cage diving with great whites (Sharklady Adventures, T 028 313 2306) and big game fishing (Two Oceans Sport Fishing Charters, T 082 460 8280). Experienced surfers can get their kicks riding the huge breakers at Dungeons reef near Hout Bay.

Many locals jog or cycle along the promenade in Sea Point, and Atlantic views can also be enjoyed from the comfort of the Twelve Apostles Spa (see p092). As for spectator sports, Cape Town has three main loves – rugby, cricket and football. For the full vuvuzela experience, look out for double-headers at Cape Town Stadium (see p010) involving the city's top clubs, Santos and Ajax, or games against Joburg's finest, Kaizer Chiefs and Orlando Pirates. Summer visitors can enjoy Test cricket at Sahara Park Newlands (opposite), and winter is the rugby season, when games are played at the nearby Newlands Stadium (8 Boundary Road, T 021 659 4600).
For full addresses, see Resources.

Sahara Park Newlands

As with many venues in Cape Town, the setting makes it. For all the English village-green gentility evoked by a well-groomed pitch and cricket whites, there's nothing like the thrusting presence of Devil's Peak looming above to lend a sense of drama to the proceedings and create what locals claim to be the most picturesque cricket ground in the world. It first hosted a Test match back in 1889 and remains a popular destination in summer (December and January), when touring international teams take on South Africa, one of the world's best sides. Tickets are often available on the day. If your visit doesn't coincide with a Test match, it's still a lovely spot to while away an afternoon watching the local club, Cape Cobras.
146 Campground Road, T 021 657 2003, www.capecobras.co.za

Sea Point Pavilion

Cape Town is surrounded by sea but little of it is swim-friendly – the Atlantic Ocean is too cold and the Indian a tiresome drive. If you're after a workout, or simply want to wet your feet, take your cossie to the iconic Sea Point Pavilion (open 7am to 7pm in summer). The current complex replaced an ugly, multi-tiered concrete structure dating back to 1913. It was built in the 1950s and has remained blissfully unchanged since then, despite often being eyed with zeal by unscrupulous developers. There are four saltwater pools, one of which is Olympic-sized. Get there early, especially in high season. A worthy alternative is the Newlands Swimming Pool (T 021 671 2729), which is graced with a lovely modernist pavilion topped by a floating, swallow-shaped canopy.
Beach Road, T 021 434 3341

091

SPORTS

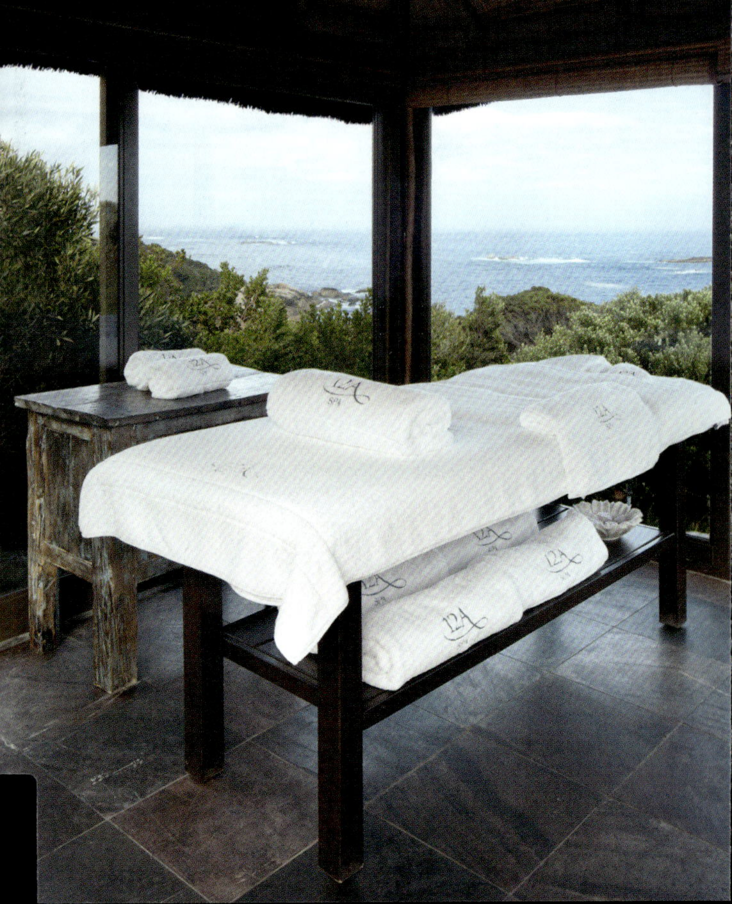

Twelve Apostles Spa

This property, stunningly located high up between Camps Bay and Llandudno, was once the source of controversy. In 1992, a Joburg ad exec sold his isolated homestead to a developer, who planned to transform it into a hotel. Locals were outraged, and models even staged a topless protest (a PR stunt for Cape Town's embryonic agencies), but councillors turned a blind eye. Any nudity now linked to the Twelve Apostles Hotel is confined to its spa. An eclectic, almost kitsch, 2012 redesign by Toni Tollman mixes Eastern ideals, vernacular icons and sea-inspired murals, and makes the most of the pristine views. Facilities include seven treatment rooms, an Arabic rasul chamber, a saltwater flotation pool and two mountain gazebos (opposite).
Victoria Road, T 021 437 9000, www.12apostleshotel.com

Muizenberg

Surfers are notoriously protective of their turf. Muizenberg, though, is where Capetonians of all persuasions learn the sport. Equipment hire and lessons can be arranged at Gary's Surf School (T 021 788 9839), which also holds sandboarding classes on the nearby dunes. Given the blustery southeaster, which can blow for days, you might want to opt for kite surfing instead – sign up for lessons at Surfstore Africa (T 021 788 5055). A chichi holiday destination in earlier years, when Agatha Christie was a notable visitor, Muizenberg is undergoing a renaissance. While you're in the area, stop off at Casa Labia (T 021 788 6062), an art gallery and café set in a restored 1929 Venetian-style mansion, on your way to check out the colourful beach huts in St James (pictured).

095

SPORTS

ESCAPES

WHERE TO GO IF YOU WANT TO LEAVE TOWN

It is by no means essential to leave Cape Town to get away from it all. There are beaches aplenty and some of South Africa's most dramatic topography right in the middle of the city. However, for those keen to explore, the coastal regions and hinterland to the north-east offer an abundance of adventure, wildlife and culinary delights. Our suggestions include some easy day-drive excursions and a safari outing that requires at least an overnight stay.

Although much of the greater Cape was intensively farmed for two centuries, conservation entrepreneurs have reintroduced 'big five' game – lion, leopard, elephant, buffalo and the increasingly endangered rhino – to their former habitat. Of these reserves, we favour Gondwana (see p102). It's a six-hour drive via the R62, a legendary back road that takes in mountain passes and the desert towns of Calitzdorp and Barrydale. Return via the Garden Route (glorious in spring) and stop for whale watching at De Hoop (T 021 422 4522, www.dehoopcollection.com), bungee jumping off the world's highest single-span arched concrete bridge (T 042 281 1458, www.faceadrenalin.com), or to chill at Godswindow (see p098).

If time is limited, don't miss the Cape winelands (see p032), just an hour or so away. Franschhoek (see p100), about 80km from Cape Town, is known for its fine cuisine, literary festival and Gallic obsession (Franschhoek translates as 'French corner').

For full addresses, see Resources.

Babylonstoren, Paarl

Set in the Drakenstein Valley, a 45-minute drive from Cape Town, Babylonstoren and its restaurant Babel is a must for foodies. The Cape Dutch homestead looks much as it did in 1777, but for the stylish interiors by designer Karen Roos. The centrepiece of the vast estate is a neatly ordered garden with 300 varieties of edible plant. You'll also find beehives, a prickly pear maze, a vineyard producing half a dozen wines and 18 types of grape, and the balauwood Puff Adder walk (above), designed by Patrice Taravella, which shades clivia lilies. Diners can pick their own food but book well ahead for lunch or supper; casual visitors can eat in the greenhouse tearoom. The hotel and spa is fastidiously white, and rooms have open hearth fires in winter.
Klapmuts/Simondium Road,
T 021 863 3852, www.babylonstoren.com

Godswindow, Swellendam
Unlike the whitewashed Cape Dutch dwellings in nearby Swellendam, South Africa's third oldest town, this modernist villa makes no bones about its ambitions: it wants to blend in with the surroundings. Designed by Joburg architect Georg van Gass and landscaped by Patrick Watson, this ultra-exclusive retreat – it has two guest rooms and a restaurant that serves by prior arrangement only – is composed of three discrete box structures that form the edges of a private courtyard. The thick masonry walls and concrete roofs create the perfect cave-like escape, with only the Langeberg Mountains to distract you. Hire a guide and go spotting for a jackal buzzard or black eagle, or hike up to the rock pools and waterfalls.
R60, Leeurivier, T 028 314 0385, www.godswindow.co.za

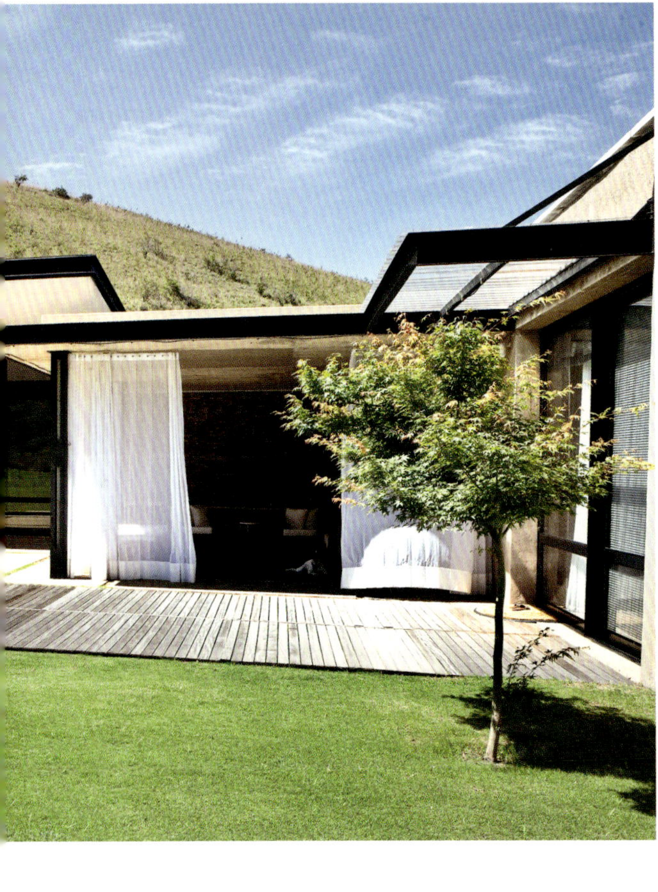

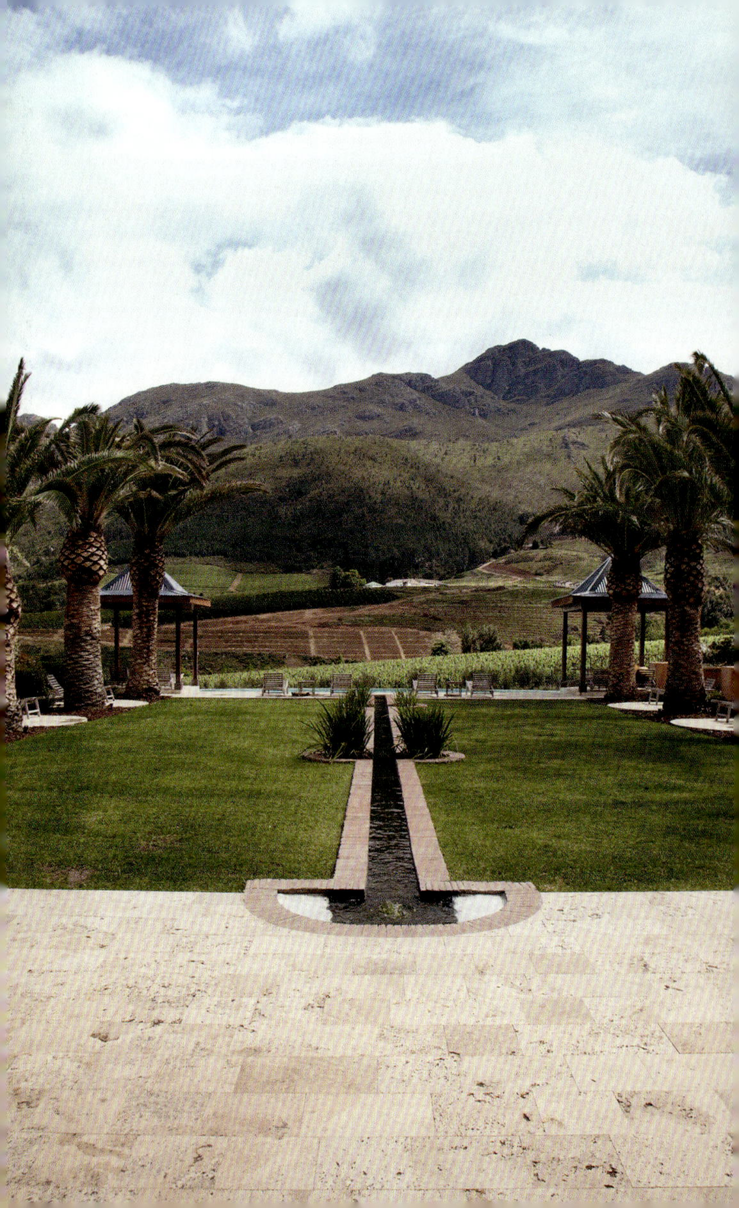

La Residence, Franschhoek

Tucked away on a working farm, this neo-rococo villa is the best way to enjoy Franschhoek's sybaritic delights. The 11 suites (Disa, above) here are decorated with chandeliers, Persian carpets and an eclectic mix of objets d'art and antiques. All boast palatial bathrooms, as well as balconies and patios with views of the estate and surrounding mountains. La Residence is a great base from which to explore the local wineries and world-class restaurants, and the hotel can also organise trout fishing, quad-biking and hot-air ballooning. Or you may just want to stay put and take advantage of the infinity pool and personalised spa treatments, before settling down to eat in the majestic baronial dining room.
Elandskloof Farm, T 021 876 4100, www.laresidence.co.za

Gondwana, Mossel Bay
This 11,000-hectare safari park near the Indian Ocean is the world's only fynbos ('fine bush' or shrubland) reserve where the big five roam freely. Overlooking valley waterholes, living quarters with round thatched roofs (Lehele Deck, pictured) are inspired by traditional Khoi-San architecture. Stay in the Kwena Lodge or an individual villa.
R327 to Herbertsdale, T 021 424 5430

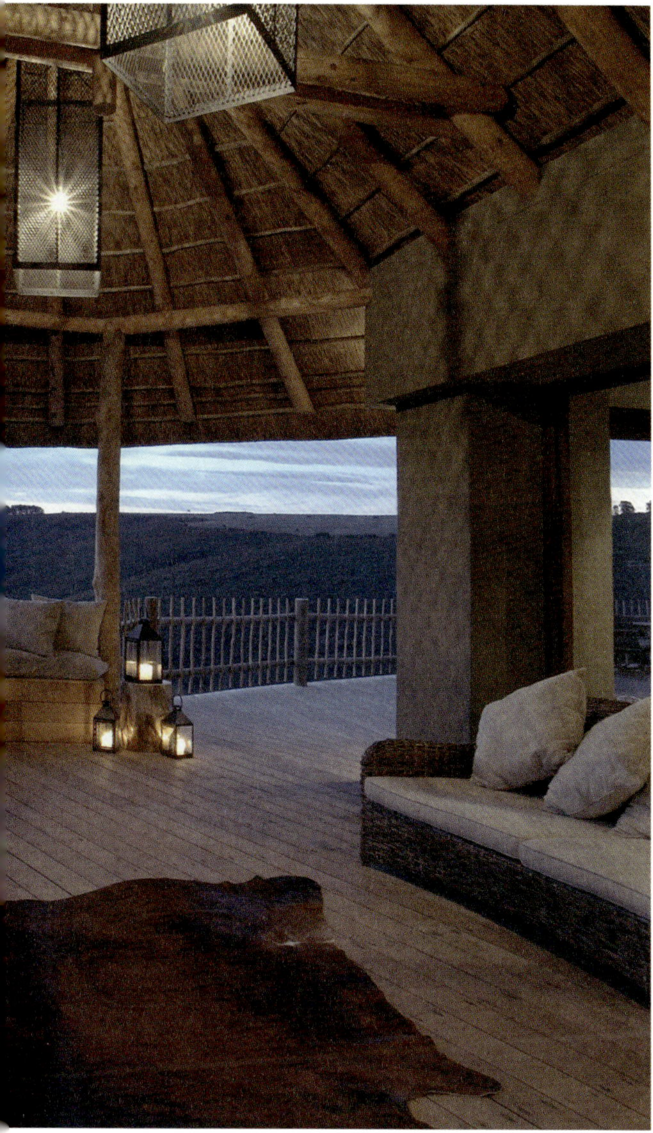

NOTES
SKETCHES AND MEMOS

RESOURCES
CITY GUIDE DIRECTORY

A
&Union 068
110 Bree Street
T 021 422 2770
www.andunion.com

Abseil Africa 088
297 Long Street
T 021 424 4760
www.abseilafrica.co.za

Adriaan Kuiters 070
73 Kloof Street
T 021 424 5502
www.adriaankuiters.com

Africa Nova 080
72 Waterkant Street
T 021 425 5123
www.africanova.co.za

African Image 080
Burg Street/Church Street
T 021 423 8385
www.african-image.co.za

B
Baxter Theatre Centre 044
Main Road
Rondebosch
T 021 685 7880
www.baxter.co.za

C
Café Caprice 047
37 Victoria Road
T 021 438 8315
www.cafecaprice.co.za

Cape Capers 078
20 Erica Street
T 021 448 3117
www.tourcapers.co.za

Cape Town Stadium 010
Vlei Road

Cape Town Tandem Paragliding 088
T 076 892 2283
www.paraglide.co.za

Carin Smuts Studio Architects 078
64 Ocean View Drive
T 021 433 1330
www.csstudio.co.za

Carne SA 054
70 Keerom Street
T 021 424 3460
www.carne-sa.com

Casa Labia 094
192 Main Road
Muizenberg
T 021 788 6062
www.casalabia.co.za

Casamento 080
160 Albert Road
T 021 448 6183
www.casamento.co.za

Castle of Good Hope 009
Castle Street
T 021 787 1260
www.castleofgoodhope.co.za

Chandler House 070
53 Church Street
T 083 423 2001

City Hall 072
Darling Street
T 021 465 2029

Civic Centre 076
12 Hertzog Boulevard
T 021 400 2303

Clarke's Bar & Dining Room 059
133 Bree Street
T 021 424 7648
www.clarkesdining.co.za

La Colombe 048
*Spaanschemat River Road
Constantia
T 021 794 2390
www.constantia-uitsig.com*
Commune1 036
*64 Wale Street
T 021 423 5600
www.commune1.com*
Customs House 072
Heerengracht Street

D
Deerpark Café 014
*2 Deer Park Avenue
T 021 462 6311*
Delaire Graff Estate 042
*R130
Helshoogte Pass
Stellenbosch
T 021 885 8160
www.delaire.co.za*
Deluxe Coffeeworks 032
*25 Church Street
T 082 681 5740
www.deluxecoffeeworks.co.za*
Disa Park Towers 014
Chelmsford Road
Downhill Adventures 088
*Shop 10
Overbeek Building
Kloof Street/Long Street/Orange Street
T 021 422 0388
www.downhilladventures.com*
The Duchess of Wisbeach 070
*3 Wisbeach Road
T 021 434 1525*

E
Earth Fair Food Market 070
*St George's Mall
www.earthfairmarket.co.za*
Eastern Food Bazaar 034
*96 Longmarket Street
T 021 461 2458
www.easternfoodbazaar.co.za*

F
Face Adrenalin 096
*T 042 281 1458
www.faceadrenalin.com*
Frazer Parfum Laboratory 081
*108 Bree Street
T 082 463 5104
www.frazerparfum.com*
Fugard 044
*Caledon Street
T 021 461 4554
www.thefugard.com*

G
Gary's Surf School 094
*34 Balmoral Building
Beach Road
Muizenberg
T 021 788 9839
www.garysurf.com*
Giovanni's 010
*103 Main Road
T 021 434 6893*
Glen Carlou Vineyards 032
*Simondium Road
Klapmuts
T 021 875 5528
www.glencarlou.co.za*

Goodman Gallery 038
*Fairweather House
176 Sir Lowry Road
T 021 462 7573
www.goodman-gallery.com*
Grand Café & Beach 058
*Granger Bay Road
Off Beach Road
T 021 425 0551
www.grandafrica.com*
Grand Café & Room 058
*35 Victoria Road
T 021 438 4253
www.grandafrica.com*
The Greenhouse 053
*The Cellars-Hohenort
93 Brommersvlei Road
T 021 794 2137
www.cellars-hohenort.com*
Guga S'Thebe Arts & Culture Centre 078
*Washington Street
Langa
T 021 695 3493*

H
Haas Collective 087
*67 Rose Street
T 021 422 4413
www.haascollective.com*
Haldane Martin 086
*Fairweather House
176 Sir Lowry Road
T 021 461 1785
www.haldanemartin.co.za*

Harbour House 066
*First floor
Kalk Bay Harbour
T 021 788 4133
www.harbourhouse.co.za*
Heath Nash 080
*2 Mountain Road
T 021 447 5757
www.heathnash.com*
Hemelhuijs 049
*71 Waterkant Street
T 021 418 2042
www.hemelhuijs.co.za*
Honest 043
*66 Wale Street
T 021 423 8762
www.honestchocolate.co.za*
De Hoop 096
*R319 to Swellendam
T 021 422 4522
www.dehoopcollection.com*

K
The Kitchen 039
*111 Sir Lowry Road
T 021 462 2201
www.karendudley.co.za*
Klûk 080
*47 Bree Street
T 083 377 7780
www.kluk.co.za*

L
Liam Mooney showroom 070
*64 Wale Street
T 770 7461
www.liammooney.co.za*

Loading Bay 082
30 Hudson Street
T 021 425 6320
www.loadingbay.co.za
Loading Bay Café 083
30 Hudson Street
T 021 425 6321
www.loadingbay.co.za

M
Manna Epicure 052
151 Kloof Street
T 021 426 2413
Mano's 070
39 Main Road
T 021 434 1090
Melissa's 012
94 Kloof Street
T 021 424 5540
www.melissas.co.za
MeMeMe 080
117a Long Street
T 021 424 0001
www.mememe.co.za
Merchants on Long 084
34 Long Street
T 021 422 2828
www.merchantsonlong.com
Milnerton Flea Market 070
Paarden Eiland
T 021 551 7879
www.milnertonfleamarket.co.za
Missibaba 080
229 Bree Street
T 021 424 8127
www.missibaba.com
Mountain Club of South Africa 088
97 Hatfield Street
T 021 465 3412
www.mcsacapetown.co.za

Mutual Building 034
14 Darling Street

N
95 Keerom 054
95 Keerom Street
T 021 422 0765
www.95keerom.com
Neighbourgoods Market 080
The Old Biscuit Mill
375 Albert Road
www.neighbourgoodsmarket.co.za
Newlands Stadium 088
8 Boundary Road
T 021 659 4600
Newlands Swimming Pool 090
Main Road/Sans Souci Road
T 021 671 2729

O
The Old Biscuit Mill 080
375 Albert Road
T 021 486 5999
www.theoldbiscuitmill.co.za
Origin Coffee 032
28 Hudson Street
www.originroasting.co.za

P
PaddleYak 088
T 044 533 0537
www.seakayak.co.za
Pedersen + Lennard 080
The Woodstock Exchange
66 Albert Road
T 021 447 2020
www.pedersenlennard.co.za

La Perla 048
Beach Road
T 021 439 9538
www.laperla.co.za
PISCO Bar 070
50 Waterkant Street
T 021 419 2633
www.pisco-bar.co.za
The Polana 066
Kalk Bay Harbour
T 021 788 7162
www.harbourhouse.co.za/polana
The Power & The Glory 050
13d Kloof Nek Road
T 021 422 2108

Q
Le Quartier Français 048
16 Huguenot Road
Franschhoek
T 021 876 2151
www.lqf.co.za

R
Railway Police Station 072
Zwaans Road
Retreat
Railway Station 072
Adderley Street
Reuben's 048
19 Huguenot Road
Franschhoek
T 021 876 3772
www.reubens.co.za
Ritz Hotel 073
Main Road/Camberwell Road
T 021 439 6010
www.cape-town-ritz-hotel.com

The Roundhouse 056
Kloof Road
The Glen
T 021 438 4347
www.theroundhouserestaurant.com
Royale Eatery 062
273 Long Street
T 021 422 4536
www.royaleeatery.com

S
6 Spin Street 067
6 Spin Street
T 021 461 0666
www.6spinstreet.co.za
St Yves Beach Club 046
The Promenade
Victoria Road
T 021 438 0826
www.styves.co.za
Sahara Park Newlands 089
146 Campground Road
T 021 657 2003
www.capecobras.co.za
Sea Point Pavilion 090
Beach Road
T 021 434 3341
Sharklady Adventures 088
T 028 313 2306
www.sharklady.co.za
Skinny LaMinx 080
201 Bree Street
T 021 424 6290
www.skinnylaminx.com
Sky Bar 070
The Village Lodge
49 Napier Street
T 021 421 1106
www.thevillagelodge.sa.com

SMAC Art Gallery 048
In-Fin Art Building
Buitengracht Street/Buitensingel Street
T 021 422 5100
www.smacgallery.com

Stevenson 038
Buchanan Building
160 Sir Lowry Road
T 021 462 1500
www.michaelstevenson.com

Superette 032
The Woodstock Exchange
66 Albert Road
T 021 802 5525
www.superette.co.za

Surfstore Africa 094
Nautilus Shopping Center
Muizenberg
T 021 788 5055
www.surfstore.co.za

T

Taal Monument 040
Gabbema Doordrift Street
Paarl Mountain
T 021 872 3441
www.taalmuseum.co.za

Table Mountain Aerial Cableway 012
Lower Cableway Station
Tafelberg Road
T 021 424 8181
www.tablemountain.net

Test Kitchen 060
Shop 104a
The Old Biscuit Mill
375 Albert Road
T 021 447 2337
www.thetestkitchen.co.za

Tokara 032
R310
Stellenbosch
T 021 808 5900
www.tokara.co.za

Top of the Ritz 073
The Ritz Hotel
Main Road/Camberwell Road
T 021 439 6988
www.cape-town-ritz-hotel.com

Truth Coffee 033
26 Buitenkant Street
T 021 200 0440
www.truthcoffee.com

Twelve Apostles Spa 092
Twelve Apostles Hotel
Victoria Road
T 021 437 9000
www.12apostleshotel.com

Two Oceans Sport Fishing Charters 088
T 082 460 8280
www.twooceanssportfishing.com

U

Usasazo Secondary School 072
7778 Bangiso Drive
Khayelitsha

W

Waterfront Boat Company 088
Shop 7
Quay 5
V&A Waterfront
T 021 418 5806
www.waterfrontboats.co.za

Waterkloof 072
*Sir Lowry's Pass Road
Somerset West
T 021 858 1292
www.waterkloofwines.co.za*
The Woodlands Eatery 064
*2 Deerpark Drive West
T 021 801 5799
www.thewoodlandseatery.co.za*
The Woodstock Exchange 080
*66-68 Albert Road
T 021 486 5999
www.woodstockexchange.co.za*

HOTELS
ADDRESSES AND ROOM RATES

Babylonstoren 097
Room rates:
double, from R4,500
Klapmuts/Simondium Road
Paarl
T 021 863 3852
www.babylonstoren.com

Boutique Manolo 026
Room rates:
suites, from R1,800;
Penthouse, from R4,000
33 Leeukloof Drive
T 021 426 2330
www.boutique-manolo.co.za

Camps Bay Retreat 022
Room rates:
suites, from R2,590:
Room One, R6,220
7 Chilworth Road
T 021 437 9703
www.campsbayretreat.com

Cape Grace 016
Room rates:
double, from R5,080
West Quay Road
T 021 410 7100
www.capegrace.com

Daddy Long Legs 024
Room rates:
double, from R975;
The Photo Booth, from R975
134 Long Street
T 021 422 3074
www.daddylonglegs.co.za

Ebb Tide 030
Room rates:
One-bedroom apartment, from R2,900;
Three-bedroom apartment, from R4,900
143 Victoria Road
T 083 719 5735
www.ebb-tide.co.za

Ellerman House & Villa 020
Room rates:
double, from R5,500;
Three-bedroom Ellerman Villa, R58,800
180 Kloof Road
T 021 430 3200
www.ellerman.co.za

Glen Beach Villas 016
Room rates:
penthouse, price on request
1 Strathmore Road
T 083 675 8266
www.glenbeachvillas.co.za

Godswindow 098
Room rates:
suite, from R2,000 (per person)
R60
Leeurivier
Swellendam
T 028 314 0385
www.godswindow.co.za

Gondwana 102
Room rates:
villa, from R600 (per person);
Kwena Lodge, R600 (per person)
R327 to Herbertsdale
Mossel Bay
T 021 424 5430
www.gondwanagr.co.za

The Grand Daddy 024
Room rates:
double, from R1,900;
Airstream trailers, from R1,900
38 Long Street
T 021 424 7247
www.granddaddy.co.za

Hout Bay Manor 028
Room rates:
double, from R1,920;
The Sotho, R4,090;
Sangoma Suite, R5,700
Baviaanskloof
Off Main Road
T 021 790 0116
www.houtbaymanor.com

Lion's View 031
Room rates:
Penthouse, R2,900;
Villa, from R5,900
4 First Crescent
T 083 719 5735
www.lionsview.co.za

Mount Nelson Hotel 016
Room rates:
double, from R3,730
76 Orange Street
T 021 483 1000
www.mountnelson.co.za

Mutual Building 034
Room rates:
Penthouse Suite, from R20,000
(two-week minimum stay)
14 Darling Street
T 021 794 3140

Pod 017
Room rates:
double, from R1,550;
Deluxe Suites, from R4,300
3 Argyle Road
T 021 438 8550
www.pod.co.za

La Residence 101
Room rates:
suites, from R5,130;
Disa Suite, from R5,130
Elandskloof Farm
Franschhoek
T 021 876 4100
www.laresidence.co.za

The Spa House 074
Room rates:
house, from R13,000
Avenue Suzanne
T 021 790 8737
www.capedreamstay.co.za

2inn1 Kensington 016
Room rates:
double, from R1,450
21 Kensington Crescent
T 021 423 1707
www.2inn1.com

Villa St Leon 072
Room rates:
villa, price on request
3a St Leon Avenue
T 021 434 6158
www.sa-venues.com

The Village Lodge 016
Room rates:
double, from R650
49 Napier Street
T 021 421 1106
www.villagelodge.co.za

WALLPAPER* CITY GUIDES

Executive Editor
Rachael Moloney

Editor
Jeremy Case
Authors
Bridget Downing
Sean O'Toole

Art Director
Loran Stosskopf
Art Editor
Eriko Shimazaki
Designer
Mayumi Hashimoto
Map Illustrator
Russell Bell

Photography Editor
Elisa Merlo
Assistant Photography Editor
Nabil Butt

Chief Sub-Editor
Nick Mee
Sub-Editor
Farah Shafiq

Editorial Assistant
Emma Harrison

Intern
Charlotte Tillieux

Wallpaper* Group Editor-in-Chief
Tony Chambers
Publishing Director
Gord Ray
Managing Editor
Oliver Adamson

Contributors
Alexander Learmonth
Nicola Sochen
Tau Tavengwa
Gabrielle Weinstein

Wallpaper* ® is a registered trademark of IPC Media Limited

First published 2007
Revised and updated 2011 and 2013

All prices are correct at the time of going to press, but are subject to change.

Printed in China

PHAIDON

Phaidon Press Limited
Regent's Wharf
All Saints Street
London N1 9PA

Phaidon Press Inc
180 Varick Street
New York, NY 10014

Phaidon® is a registered trademark of Phaidon Press Limited

www.phaidon.com

A CIP Catalogue record for this book is available from the British Library.

All rights reserved. No part of this publication may be reproduced, stored in a retrieval system or transmitted, in any form or by any means, electronic, mechanical, photocopying, recording or otherwise, without the prior permission of Phaidon Press.

© 2007, 2011 and 2013
IPC Media Limited

ISBN 978 0 7148 6613 0

PHOTOGRAPHERS

Susan Bockelmann and Dennis Gilbert
Cape Town city view, inside front cover
Cape Town Stadium, pp010-011
Pod, p017, pp018-019
The Grand Daddy, p024, p025
Boutique Manolo, pp026-027
Stevenson, p038
The Kitchen, p039
Carne SA, pp054-055
The Roundhouse, pp056-057
Test Kitchen, pp060-061
Royale Eatery, p062, p063
&Union, pp068-069
Merchants On Long, pp084-085

Sophie Corben
La Residence, p100, p101

Christopher Floyd
Taal Monument, pp040-041

Andries Joubert
Godswindow, pp098-099

Hamish Niven
Ebb Tide, pp030-031

Peartree Digital
Frazer Parfum, p081

Alain Proust
Babylonstoren, p097

David Southwood
Table Mountain, p012
Rhodes Memorial, p013
Disa Park Towers, pp014-015
Mutual Building, pp034-035
Harbour House, p066
Ritz Hotel, p073
Guga S'Thebe Arts & Culture Centre, pp078-079
Sahara Park Newlands, p089
Beach huts, St James, pp094-095

Jac de Villiers
Camps Bay Retreat, pp022-023
Hout Bay Manor, p028, p029
Truth Coffee, p033
Commune 1, p036, p037
Honest, p043
St Yves Beach Club, p046, p047
Hemelhuijs, p049
The Power & The Glory, pp050-051
Manna Epicure, p052
The Greenhouse, p053
Clarke's Bar & Dining Room, p059
The Woodlands Eatery, pp064-065
Liam Mooney, p071
The Spa House, pp074-075
Loading Bay, p082, p083
Haldane Martin, p086
Haas Collective, p087
Sea Point Pavilion, pp090-091
Twelve Apostles Spa, p092, p093

Jonathan de Villiers
Baxter Theatre Centre, pp044-045

Pam Warne
6 Spin Street, p067

CAPE TOWN
A COLOUR-CODED GUIDE TO THE HOT 'HOODS

ATLANTIC SEABOARD
Designer homes and lively bars and eateries nestle between the mountains and the sea

GREEN POINT
The focal point of redevelopment for the World Cup boasts much more than its stadium

CENTRE
Long Street is the city's main drag and its restaurants and clubs will keep you coming back

WATERFRONT/LOWER CITY
The slick V&A marina is a tourist magnet; the architecture of the CBD is more interesting

WOODSTOCK
Art galleries and independent retail are gentrifying this area towards the hip side of edgy

CITY BOWL SUBURBS
Sought-after real estate spreads out from Kloof Street's upmarket stores and nightlife

For a full description of each neighbourhood, see the Introduction.
Featured venues are colour-coded, according to the district in which they are located.